From Anger To Enlightenment

A Survivor's Story of Faith

I never truly lived until I lived no more

ROBERT PALASCIANO

Contact at FromAngerToEnlightenment@gmail.com

Published by AJS Publishing, Plainview, New York

Cover Art by SelfPubBookCovers.com

Print Design-Layout by Lorie DeWorken, Mind the Margins, LLC

Author photograph by Adam Palasciano

Visit the website at www.FromAngerToEnlightenment.net

Website Design by Terry Gallogly, miniMAX Corp.

ISBN 978-0-9907203-0-0

Library of Congress Control Number: 2014915373

First Edition

CONTENTS

INTRODUCTION

My name is Robert Julius Palasciano and I was murdered on November 29, 1990, the 333rd day of the year. The following chronicle is a factual account of how I died and journeyed to Heaven, the Most Glorious Place. In Heaven, I met Our Lady of Mercy, who saved me from a tragic death and gave me a wondrous gift with a message. Then She returned me to live once more. This is my story of personal revelation. It's led me to understand the mystery of why Our Lady saved and sent me back. This book is about the questions we ask of God and why they aren't answered as quickly and painlessly as we would like them to be. Perhaps, He allows us to endure hatred to understand what love truly is; to bear tremendous pain so we can fathom the ecstasy of life. This story is about faith, lost and found. It's beautiful but it's also horrific, and I wouldn't have it any other way.

My journey for understanding has taken more than twenty years, and my goal is to share the wisdom I've gained to help survivors of traumatic events. I'm not a doctor. I'm an ordinary person who's experienced extraordinary events. I believe after twenty three years of coping through the various stages of mental trauma, that I've developed a certain expertise. I've learned how to relieve the pain and suffering that it brings to us. Specifically, I've learned how to relieve my powerful negative feelings of guilt and anger. I have also found new weapons against the influences of our devastating nightmares and I'd like to share all that I've learned with you. Since I returned from Heaven, more than twenty years ago, I've been guided down many tributaries and given many pieces of life changing wisdom. Together these experiences have coalesced into a magnificent understanding of my purpose in life.

If you're like me, then your mind also suffers from the evil that touched you when you were traumatized by another. Do you experience waking flashbacks and nightmares so vivid that you can't function during the day as you once did? Does your mental fortitude crumble from even the slightest stress? If so, I invite you to listen to my *Survivor's Story of Faith* which has taken me all the way *From Anger to Enlightenment*.

My journey began twenty three years ago, born of an unsavory encounter with the Olive Skinned Man. For years, I strove to pen my thoughts into a body of work to make sense of it all. Each attempt however, was prejudiced by a caldera of pent up rage festering inside me. My clouded perception corrupted each version and I trashed them, one after another. My purpose and direction weren't yet clear, until one day.

In 2012, my doctor asked me to host a meeting for a panel of experienced psychiatrists about my experiences with what they call Post Traumatic Stress Disorder or PTSD. My doctor felt the panel might gain treatment insight from my personal experience with the condition. Naturally, I was dumbfounded.

I thought how could a group of distinguished psychiatrists gain any insight into this stress related condition from me? Weren't they the ones with all the experience and answers? I accepted his invitation hoping I could somehow learn from their combined knowledge and experience. I had no idea it would be the other way around.

On one particular day, I met with the panel of psychiatrists. They asked me many questions about my experiences and how my symptoms have disrupted my once normal life. I explained to them how waking flashbacks feel and how they affect the mind, even hours after the event. I explained how our brutal nightmares and constant state of hyper-vigilance changes how we think and what we feel at the core of our personality. They asked me if faith has helped my recovery in any way. I went on to tell them how faith saved me from death and has been a significant weapon in the defense against this stress related condition.

I have to admit, reliving those stories again was traumatizing. I was cold and sweaty and my heart was pounding furiously. My hands trembled so much I couldn't even drink a cup of water without spilling it on myself. Yet despite this obvious downside, there was an equally but less obvious upside. These experienced doctors all told me how astonished they were by my impressive personal perspective. They felt that I explained this condition in a way they have never heard before. In fact, as a result, they suggested that they record our next session for use in training medical residents of trauma patients. They also suggested I lead a support group for trauma victims in the area. It honestly surprised me that these experienced doctors could learn anything from me. At the same time I realized that I could help other survivors of trauma. So began my mission to write a book about how anyone can conquer the degenerative psychological effects of the condition which I call *Trauma Induced Stress*.

I believe the term Trauma Induced Stress more appropriately describes how we survivors feel. I believe this term removes the negative connotation of the word disorder. We've been induced with stress through traumatic events. We didn't catch this condition; rather it was inflicted on us. Our minds have been induced with stress as a consequence of our own particular brand of trauma. Some survivors experienced these events in a protracted abusive childhood. Other survivors are imposed with this condition because of war or violent crime. In every case of Trauma Induced Stress, something important was torn away from us, which we may never get back. We've lost our innocence, our sense of safety, and our belief that we didn't deserve what came of us. We survivors feared and may continue to fear our own imminent death. Many more of us have lost body parts, the effects of which traumatize us every day.

Any of us may incur this condition by events which may occur from childhood to adulthood. I believe our suffering may be long-lasting, especially if the events were extreme or protracted. When our symptoms hold us down, we feel powerless and alone. Few can understand how we can be so affected by events that took place long ago. Those people expect time to heal our wounds, but it doesn't. Believe me, I felt just like you for so many years, but a new age has dawned, one of understanding and enlightenment. Despite our daily dose of unwanted guilt, anger, flashbacks, and nightmares, we'll always remember that we're survivors before all else. My fellow survivors please understand that you are NOT alone, for we are many and help is here.

This book accepts anger and guilt as a natural consequence of Trauma Induced Stress, and teaches forgiveness as a permanent cure. It's been twenty three years since my trip to Heaven and my visit with Our Lady of Mercy. I now understand my purpose is to deliver a message. Please listen to these words, because I believe it's only through God's love that we will reach this existence in Heaven. All He asks of us is that we believe in Him and love one another as we would love Him. Through my suffering, I've gained a perspective of enlightenment which I must share with other survivors. I know in my heart I was meant to bring peace to those who've suffered as I have. *I'll always remember and cherish the time I spent in Heaven, and I'll never fear death when it comes to me again, for I know that it's only the beginning.* For now, there's much work to do in this life.

Chapter One

JUDGMENT DAY

*Enlightenment is illusive and can only be received
by those who ask for it and by those who are worthy to receive it.
Only then will you be shown the path.*

My mind swiftly drifted into shades of darkness, as the resonance of a high pitched and continuous beeping reverberated inside my brain, sending me back... The sound was so reminiscent of my heart monitor in the ICU and dragged me back even further than cared to go, to a place reserved only for the dying and the dead. Steel, cold steel embedded into my flesh, and I lay counting and re-counting the metallic impingements, one, two, three, then ten, then twenty... Each expansion of my lungs drove writhing pain through every tender nerve, resulting in endless agonizing screams.

My right hand inched its way over to touch the cold stainless steel surgical staples buried into my torso, and holding my guts from pouring out. Sunk deep into my hospital bed and even deeper into my own misery, I lay writhing in torturous agony. The horrid necessity of breathing forced oxygen from the mechanical ventilator was long overcome by the excruciating pain that each breath created. Unable to manufacture a scream, I screamed on the inside, that is, when I wasn't crying or thinking how death would somehow end my suffering. But even worse than that, thinking of how my murderer had yet gone unpunished.

The high frequency beeping manufactured by a nearby sanitation truck ceased, and suddenly I snapped out of my ghastly flashback and returned to my day. I have never gotten over how this simple yet powerful sound continues still to mimic the resonant signature of the hospital room in which I remained for 77 days and which continues to drag me back into my personal Hell.

For years I've lingered with unwavering expectation, waiting patiently for the opportunity to exact my revenge on the Olive Skinned Man. Driven by fury and fueled by frenzy, I planned my retribution down to the finest detail. Only one-piece of the puzzle was missing, the Olive Skinned Man. I always thought when I ultimately found him, that I'd be vigilant in studying his daily patterns and movements. Before I struck, I'd stalk him, just as he stalked me. Like a shadow, I'd follow him everywhere he went. I'd patiently find out where he lived, worked, and socialized, taking comfort in the knowledge that my revenge would be sweet.

The air was crisp and dry and on one particular autumn day, I found myself in Bayside, Queens. After closing a big sale, I had a huge appetite and a craving for a succulent Porterhouse steak. The Porterhouse is actually two steaks in one, a New York Strip and a Fillet Mignon. It's like a T-bone steak only bigger and with more fillet relative to strip. I began to leisurely walk north up Bell Boulevard toward Uncle Jack's, one of my favorite steakhouses. I could smell the aroma of incredible deliciousness wafting in my direction.

I approached the restaurant and noticed a man getting out of a white van from across the street. He began to cross Bell Boulevard and started walking my way. I glanced at him and noticed there was something eerily familiar about him. He stepped from the street to the sidewalk and we were now only a few yards apart. As he approached, I was overcome by the same feeling of terror I experienced on that fateful day. It felt like time slowed down fivefold, and as he crossed directly in front of my view, I saw the same olive skinned visage of evil from all those years before.

I suddenly became overwhelmed by a wave of panic, which enveloped my entire body. My heart rate rose dramatically and my legs began to shake, making it difficult to stand up. As I clutched a window ledge, I saw the Olive Skinned Man enter the same steak house that I was going toward. As I fell to my knees on the sidewalk, I became enveloped by a powerful flashback of gunshots and blood. The visual impact of the muzzle flash and the audible shock of exploding gunpowder inside the shell casing forced me to shudder and retract. The tactile ooze of my own warm blood spewing down my torso felt as real as the day it first occurred.

It took ten minutes before I overcame the powerful effects of this flashback. I cleared my head and instantly knew there was only one action I could possibly take to end my living nightmare. For countless years, I pondered the day I'd finally face the man who indelibly altered my life with the squeeze of his trigger. Although the years gave me ample time to devise multiple scenarios, the feeling of finding him, was nothing that I could've possibly imagined.

If it was truly him, what should I do next? I knew for sure that no one could ever find out about my terrible secret, locked away forever in the darkest recesses of my soul. After composing myself, I walked up and down the sidewalk, keeping a close eye on the Olive Skinned Man, who was sitting at the bar and drinking a glass of beer. It was 12:46 on a Friday afternoon, and I crossed over the street to check out his white van. I took a pad out of my suit jacket pocket and jotted down the license plate number. It was a New York commercial plate, and posted on the van's side panel was the name of a local oil company. So far I knew where he worked, and at least one place where he drank. If it was him, I also knew that he was extremely dangerous and could be carrying a gun.

I prepared myself to follow him when he left the bar, so I quickly ran down the block to get my own car. To remain inconspicuous, I parked on the street, five spaces behind the white van and I waited. As I sat there fueled by my anger, I devised a plan to inflict on him as much pain as he inflicted on me, and ending with his merciless death.

This hideous side of me, born from spilled crimson blood and gun smoke, required revenge. The evil which was passed on to me, felt like a terrible monster, trying desperately to escape its cage. I've always strived to live the life of a decent and honorable person. I'm horribly conflicted though with this dreadful beast that dwells in the deepest recesses of my heart and mind. I thought that even if I called the police, I knew the statute of limitations on his crimes had expired years ago, and he'd go free. I could only pray to God, hoping that He'd understand what I was about to do. Why else would He plan my serendipitous encounter with the Olive Skinned Man? He surely knew that it offered me the perfect opportunity to exact my deadly and final act of retribution.

In my haste I figured my best chance wasn't to wait, but rather to act in the moment. If this opportunity slipped through my grasp, it might never present itself again. I had years to mentally prepare and I already had the details of my plan worked out. I still wasn't absolutely sure it was the same Olive Skinned Man from my past, and I knew that confirming his identity would be the final step before enacting my plan. I kept a bottle of prescription Xanax in the console of my truck that I once used to reduce anxiety. I knew 10mg of Xanax combined with the alcohol he was already consuming would surely knock him unconscious long enough to drive him to a remote location. Then, I'd pay him back with my own brand of justice.

I planned to crush the pills up into a fine powder and to covertly deposit it into his glass of beer, possibly when he visited the men's room. During moments of clarity when the rage which consumed me subsided, I remember saying, "How can I be thinking of killing someone, even if he is a monster"? After all, I'm the victim, not the killer; I'm good, not evil. Yet, I was overwhelmed with fury and ruled by my evil doppelganger, created by the Olive Skinned Man. So I continued with my plan for revenge. I believed the only way to kill the monster inside me was to kill the monster that created it!

I knew that once I entered the restaurant, that I'd be taking a chance he could recognize me, so in an attempt at disguise I put on a pair of sunglasses. As I sat in my car, I thought how it might unfold. I'd sit at the bar near the Olive Skinned Man to make certain that he was truly the monster that entered my life those many years ago. I'd surely recognize him from his face and the unmistakable two inch long scar on his right hand, located between his index finger and thumb. I'd buy a beer and pay in cash, so as not to leave a paper trail. After he became drowsy from the drugs I would slip him, I'd masquerade as the Good Samaritan and help him walk out of the bar, offering to drop him off. My leather driving gloves would preclude any fingerprints. Then I'd place him unconscious in the back seat of my truck and conceal him with the blue beach blanket I always carry in the back.

I'd remove his keys from his pocket along with his wallet and cell phone, and relocate his van eight blocks away onto a main intersection. I'd position it directly in front of a convenience store. I'd be sure to leave the keys in the ignition, the windows rolled down, and the side door of the van wide open. This would expose the valuable equipment and make it a prime candidate for car theft. Finally, I'd leave his wallet and cell phone on the dashboard, making it too tempting for a thief to pass up. If the car thieves did their job well, the police would surely find it in a different neighborhood, making their search for clues more difficult. It would also offer car theft as an explanation for his disappearance. In addition, any unknown fingerprints on his van, wallet, or cell phone would offer the authorities a false trail to follow.

Then I'd walk back to my car and begin to drive upstate into the mountains. I'd remain vigilant by wearing sunglasses and a baseball cap to obscure my face, and drive within the posted speed limit to avoid attracting attention. To lessen my electronic trail, I'd pay for tolls with cash and remove the battery from within my own cell phone to disable the GPS chip until I returned home. When I was clear of the city, I'd find a secluded place and stop the car. Next, I'd unpack a roll of duct tape, which I kept in the event of a water hose leak, and use it to bind his mouth, hands, and feet. Then I'd make a quick pit stop to buy the last elements to put the finishing touches on my plan, salted peanuts and peanut butter. I'd then shift my truck into 4-wheel drive and take it off-road, going deep into to woods, and far from where anyone could see us.

At dusk, I'd take the monster out of my truck and duct tape him directly to a twisted oak tree. I'd attach his body to the twisted oak in a seated position, straddling the tree, and taping his arms and legs around it. I'd use the utility knife from my emergency tool box to cut away all his clothes, stripping him bare. When he finally woke up naked, tied to a twisted tree in the frigid dead of night, he'd know why he was there.

The end to my means wasn't acquiring a confession or eliciting an apology, it was purely for revenge. I'd incise hundreds of small wounds around his face, back, legs, and arms. I'd take great care not to sever any major arteries or veins, such as the femoral artery found in the leg, or the jugular vein which is easily accessible from the neck. My objective would be to create a strong blood scent, which would attract the indigenous predators such as the black bear, bobcat, and coyote. I knew that during this time of year, black bears were in a hyperphagia stage of gorging themselves with excess calories just before hibernation. I also recalled that a bear's sense of smell is seven times greater than a bloodhound's, and that they can sniff out a meal up to 20 miles upwind.

The proverbial icing on the cake would be peanut butter smeared all over his body. As an added scent for the animals I'd shove as many salted peanuts as I could into each raw incision. Aside from the pain caused by the salt, I knew the animals would love to eat those tasty morsels, along with his flesh. My objective was to torture him just as he had tortured me. And then I'd leave him to die, cold and alone, just as he had left me.

In case he escaped from his bindings, I'd cut through each of his Achilles tendons, located at the posterior of each ankle. This would ensure the Olive Skinned Man never left the woods alive. In the unlikely event of such an escape, I calculated he'd die anyway from exposure, as the surrounding temperature would soon dip below 45°F. After cutting off each of his fingers to remove his identity, I'd make a fire and burn his clothes and fingers, along with my own bloody leather gloves. Before leaving the area, I'd drive to a nearby lake and throw the utility knife into its depths.

When I finally return home, I'd dispose of all my clothes including my shoes and have my car detailed, inside and out. I knew I'd have to throw out my tires and pay cash for a new and different set, which I'd buy from an auto shop many miles from my home. The only trace I'd leave behind would be a set of untraceable tire tracks leading away from an unidentifiable half eaten and rotting corpse.

I was about to face my nemesis, my personal anti-Christ. Except today would be his judgment day. It was a good day for revenge, so I stepped out of my truck, crossed Bell Boulevard and entered the restaurant. I sat down at the bar stool next to the Olive Skinned Man and ordered a beer. Although many years had passed since we last met, I was sure I could recognize him. As I surveyed his features, I noted that his dark eyes were the same color, and his nose and chin were the same shape. I gasped from deep within the hollows of my chest, and then I picked up my beer glass and took a swallow.

From where I was sitting, I saw his right hand tucked into the pocket of his dark blue work pants. I thought that was odd behavior sitting at a bar, and I began to wonder if he recognized me and was clutching a pistol inside his pocket. Suddenly, the Olive Skinned Man turned in my direction, looked directly at me, and said "Hello". My heart skipped a beat but I thought that I'd play along. As I returned his greeting, he told me that his name was Anthony. I lied and told him that mine was Alex, and as I did, he extended his left hand to shake mine. Instinctively, I held out my right hand and immediately felt awkward trying to shake his left hand. I instantly remembered that the Olive Skinned Man from my past was also left handed. I thought this might be further evidence that it was in fact him. As we shook hands, the Olive Skinned Man sensed my discomfort and offered an explanation to why he couldn't shake with his right hand. I wasn't ready for what happened next.

The Olive Skinned Man slowly slid his right hand out of his pant pocket, revealing his deformed right hand. Anthony explained that because of a congenital birth defect, he couldn't shake with his right hand. For a moment I was speechless. I took a minute to adjust to my increased frustration, realizing that he wasn't the same malicious man from my past. I sunk deeper into my pit of anger knowing that my pain would have to continue, at least for now. As I stood up from the bar stool to leave the restaurant, Anthony stopped me and offered to buy me a beer. I figured it must be God's plan, albeit a cruel one. Why would God arrange this encounter with a man who I thought was the Olive Skinned Man? And just when I tried to escape my misery, why would He have this man pull me back in and buy me a drink?

I reluctantly accepted his offer and sat back down. As we drank, Anthony told me that he never felt disabled. He told me he felt like a survivor and that he believed he was blessed by God to be special. He said, "God only gave me one good hand so I would appreciate it more." I asked Anthony why he was sharing some of the most intimate details of his life with a stranger, but I didn't expect his response. He peered straight into my eyes and replied, "You look like you're in pain and need to listen to how God has brought joy into my life. My one good hand gives me perspective to understand what is truly important." He paused and we both took a drink of beer. The restaurant was busy and noisy, but I focused all my attention on Anthony as he continued to speak. "You look like you're also missing a part of yourself, and I hope my story helps you find your own true perspective."

I was overcome with emotion and could hardly compose myself. My face became twisted as I tried to hold back the urge to cry. When Anthony looked into my eyes, it felt like he knew me forever. It was like his vision penetrated the depths of my immortal soul. I instantly remembered feeling the same sensation from the slim stranger with long hair who came to my hospital room years before. I knew at that moment that Anthony's presence on this day was no coincidence. I thanked him for his kind words and left the bar. As I drove home, a sense of serenity overwhelmed me like I hadn't felt since my visit to the Most Beautiful Place.

I never expected Anthony to be such a kind and honest man. I thought, *could this be a chance encounter or rather divine intervention? Perhaps God sent Anthony here to save me from myself.* I've always believed that retribution was the sole means to rid myself of the anger within me. Although the true solution was in my grasp the entire time, I couldn't see it. I realize now that my brutal anger was the cause of my clouded perception. For years I believed my anger insulated me gave me strength. Do you believe your anger insulates you and gives you strength?

Chapter Two

FROM THE ARMS OF AN ANGEL

For nearly half my life I've searched for a man, a singular individual who changed my life forever. His actions took the previous twenty seven years of my life and all that I was, and ostensibly flipped it one hundred and eight degrees in the opposite direction. So, for the past twenty three years I've searched for him, wherever I went. Over time, the purpose of my search has drastically changed. It began as a hunt of vengeance, but over time it became transformed.

I've since gained a deep understanding of the Olive Skinned Man and the motivation that drove him. This new understanding resulted in a paradigm shift deep inside what I believe to be my soul. I now believe the purpose of my search has shifted from revenge to forgiveness and understanding, making the title inexorably, *From Anger to Enlightenment*.

When I chose the title, it didn't occur to me that it was an acronym for the word *fate*. When I realized it weeks later, I knew the title was inescapable. Fate is the power that controls events in the future. Fate is inevitable and its consequence can range from neutral to the unimaginable. The events dictated by fate are ultimately predetermined by a much higher power than us. Did fate send me on this whirlwind journey from here to Heaven and back, spanning every feeling between agony and ecstasy, or is simple coincidence responsible? Did fate drive me to pen my story, or was it purely a fluke? You decide.

I was born on The Feast of St. Patrick in the year 1963, but *I never truly lived until I lived no more.* My name is Robert Julius Palasciano and I was shot and killed on November 29, 1990, the 333rd day of the year. That day, which altered the course my life, began completely unremarkable. I woke up at 6:30 a.m., showered and prepared three fried eggs with a toasted English muffin and a cup of strong coffee. On this particular morning I planned to attend a Branch Mangers meeting with my bosses Edward O'Donnell and Richard Crowley. Mr. O'Donnell was a Vice President and responsible for a region of branches in Nassau County. Mr. Crowley was a Senior Vice President and responsible for Retail Branch Banking for all of Long Island, NY.

In my absence, my Assistant Manager, would have opened the branch that day. But during breakfast she called me at home and told me she wasn't feeling well and wouldn't be able to work. Okay change of plan, so I'd open the branch and let my Mr. O'Donnell know that I'd be late to the meeting. Could this unscheduled change be coincidence, or the work of a higher power?

I'd only been with The Bank of New York® for about five months and I wanted to look my best. I dressed in my sharpest black pinstripe suit, red silk tie and white shirt. I've never been much for wearing jewelry, so I put on a modest watch and a gold tie tack that my brother Tom gave me. It looked like rings of encircled gold broached in the center by a single diamond. And because of its sentimental value, it was my most precious piece of jewelry.

It was going to be another great day at work. My mind was clear and my body was strong and well rested. I worked out in the gym five days a week, and in six months I added ten pounds of fresh muscle. Despite my rigorous work schedule it was something I felt I needed to do, but didn't know why. I did know that I was in the best shape of my life, and I felt incredible.

I put on my overcoat and got into one of the sharpest cars I have ever owned, a 1987 Mitsubishi Starion ESI-R. It was black on black with bucket leather seats and a turbo charged engine. So I cleared the frost from the windshield and drove to my office. I was the Branch Manager of the Garden City Park branch for The Bank of New York®, located at 2131 Jericho Turnpike. I loved my job, looked up to my bosses and always tried to make a good impression. As Manager, I felt responsible for everything that happened in my branch, good or bad.

Working on Long Island was a big change for me from my previous job on Wall Street in New York City. Working in Manhattan at 30 Wall Street was exiting, but I didn't care much for the constant interruption from robberies and the occasional riot. Before I joined The Bank of New York®, I worked for The Seamen's Bank for Savings. I was the Sales Manager for three branches including their flagship Wall Street office, Beaver Street, and Pine Street. Bank robbers hit one these three branches every three weeks. Some robbed by scamming customers from right inside the bank. Others robbed by passing holdup notes to the tellers. Others still committed violent armed robberies with pistols and shotguns.

One maniac even robbed our Wall Street branch with a shoebox, which he claimed contained a bomb with a remote detonator. Fortunately, I was never on the receiving end, but my friends and co-workers were. One summer afternoon hundreds of protesters marched on Wall Street. Within minutes, there was a full-blown riot right outside my front door. When the riot became violent, I had to lock the front doors and post a security guard at the side entrance. I'd already been in banking for almost ten years, but I never saw so many robberies and violence until then. So accepting a challenging position as a Branch Manager in Long Island clearly had its advantages. I now had the opportunity the run my own branch and leave the proclivities of the lawless behind.

I arrived at my branch in Garden City Park at 7:45 a.m., with security on my mind. As usual I was the first employee to open and enter the bank. I parked behind the branch and inspected the backdoor for tampering. Ambush was always a possibility, especially if you were alone. With the back door clear I walked along the sidewalk to the front of the building and opened the first set of doors. I walked into the alcove and locked the first set of doors behind me. This prevents anyone from forcibly following me into the bank. Then I looked inside the bank for anything out of the ordinary, but it was quiet.

I opened banks hundreds of times before today, but with the second set of locked doors straight ahead, a powerful and controlling feeling came over me. It felt like something was terribly wrong but I didn't know what. This was the first time I ever felt this way and it was screaming DON'T GO IN THE BANK! I held the keys in my right hand, frozen to place them into the final lock. I waited, then waited some more. I stood motionless for ten minutes in the chilly alcove, looking to spot anything out of place.

The Vault Room looked okay and the alarm was still on. I could see the teller's area and the main lobby and it was quiet. Directly to my right I saw the bank platform, which included three desks for the Assistant Manager, Customer Service and my own. So far everything seemed in place, and I had no reason not to enter the bank. Yet, I couldn't shake that feeling telling me something was wrong. Of course my responsibility as Manager was overriding. As I finally slid the key into the keyhole, the vibrations against the tumblers ran through my fingers. I remember hearing the sound of a sharp click as I turned and opened this lock for the last time. So at last I entered the bank and dismissed the feelings I had. I cleared all the rooms that I couldn't see from the door as well as the lower level and bathrooms. Everything felt normal, and as I wound myself up expecting a busy day, those feeling washed away.

The next and most important step in any bank branch opening is setting the All-Clear Signal. The All-Clear Signal prevents employee ambush, and it's only used before the bank opening at 9:00 a.m. It lets every bank employee know whether it's safe to enter the building. Every employee knows, if the All-Clear isn't visible, don't go inside. It's any visible marker chosen in advance and seen by the employees from the street. Sometimes it's the interest rate sign or a chair moved in a particular place on the floor. Other times we'll change it and set one window blind either open or closed.

On this particular Thursday, the All-Clear Signal was the interest rate sign positioned in front of the doors. Easy right, I was a pro at opening banks and I did it hundreds of time without a single hitch. Yet, something was still influencing me and I couldn't recognize it. Then the telephone rang and I answered it. It was a woman asking to speak with Alexander Hamilton. I immediately recognized my Teller Manager's voice and realized that she didn't see the All-Clear Signal which I accidentally neglected to place by the door.

In a true ambush I'd say, Mr. Hamilton isn't in now but I'll let him know you called. Of course Alexander Hamilton, who founded The Bank of New York® in 1784, and who was also the first U.S. Secretary of the Treasury, wasn't calling anyone back. I told her, "There's no ambush. It's safe to come in." She said I was testing her, but I wasn't. It was something else. So I placed the All-Clear Signal in front of the doors and let her in the bank. She was still a little confused about what had just happened, and honestly so was I.

It was a Thursday, and my staff consisted of a Senior Customer Service Representative, a Teller Manager, and six tellers. The Customer Service Rep. worked with me on the bank platform opening new accounts and resolving client issues. I liked her from the moment I met her. She's a unique individual who is thoughtful, strong willed, and decisive. She immediately impressed me with her knowledge of banking and her ability to follow through with customer support. I suppose these extraordinary qualities came from a lifetime of experience, given she had a few years on me.

The Teller Manager had been recently promoted because she deserved the job. I instantly recognized her as an aggressive hard worker who had the knowledge and sense of responsibility to help me run the branch at almost every turn. Her lack of confidence was merely a sign of her inexperience, but I made a point to cultivate her confidence by challenging her with new responsibilities. I pushed her and expected more, but only because I knew she could handle it and deserved a role as an Assistant Branch Manager.

Once she was in the building, we unlocked the main vault and prepared for a busy day. The main vault is on the south end of the bank, so as you walk in, it's on your left. The vault secured our supply of strapped cash, rolled coin, Bank Checks, Money Orders, and Travelers Checks. It also protected the private valuables inside our client's safety deposit boxes.

There were six layers of security protecting these valuables. The first layer was a locked bullet resistant enclosure surrounding the main vault. There was an alarm designed to detect any unauthorized entry. The steel alloy vault door weighed several tons, was two-feet thick and armed with a dual four digit combination lock. In addition, the vault had a time lock that prevented opening before the appointed time. In other words, even if you had the keys to the bank, the alarm code and the vault combinations, the vault door wouldn't open until the time lock ran out. The fifth layer fortifying the main vault was an iron gate with a keyed entry. This gate also remained locked during business hours when the main vault door was open. Contrary to the way movies portray bank vaults, we didn't pile stacks of cash on a table on the middle of the room. Once inside the main vault, currency, coin, and checks had their own compartments, secured under dual control by a set of two combination locks.

It was 8:15 a.m., we were about to open the keyed entryway to the vault area when I stopped in my tracks to ponder the strange events of earlier that morning. I paused for a second and realized I was too busy to waste time thinking about my unexplained feelings, especially when I had a bank to run. When we entered the vault room I punched the code to disarm the vault alarm, 8-1-4-9. The green light came on signaling we were clear to unlock the main vault door. I spun the main dial to clear it, then started my combination, left to 19, right to 75, left to 19, and finally right to 53. Then I turned the huge wheel on the door to detract the massive metal locking cylinders extending from the door into the surrounding frame.

Unlocking and opening the enormous vault door felt awesome and it never got old. Man did I love my job. Incredibly, it only took one strong tug on the massive door and it began to open easily. Once it began moving, the door was so well-balanced that it only needed a few fingers to open. Once inside, the Teller Manager spun the upper combination to the cash vault and I spun the lower combination to complete the sequence, left to 1, right to 7, and left to 48. That was the last time I ever spun a combination on a bank vault.

Thursdays were a payroll day. We expected a few hundred workers to come in and cash their payroll checks drawn from local businesses, who were also my customers. Since these workers were living hand to mouth, they didn't have direct deposit of payroll or even a bank account for that matter. Everyone, including would-be-thieves, knew that check cashing days meant there'd be long lines and a load of cash. The check cashing rush started about 11:30 and ran through most of the afternoon.

Every Wednesday, we received an armored shipment of cash to prepare us for check cashing and regular bank business for the following week. So on November 28th, I accepted an armored shipment of about $250,000 in mixed denominations and secured it in the main vault. When we opened for business that unforgettable Thursday morning, there was about $100,000 inside the teller's unit. A bullet resistant enclosure, spanning from the counter to the ceiling, protected the teller's unit. The only entrance was a keyed doorway, and only the Teller Manager and I had keys.

With everything prepared and everyone in place, we opened the doors at 9:00 a.m., to start the day. Four customers entered the bank and headed for the tellers. I was sitting at my desk preparing to open a new business account with a $50,000 check that I picked up the night before. One of my primary roles as Manager was to increase revenue through sales of new business accounts and services. A few minutes had passed and I noticed that three of the customers had left the bank, leaving one male customer at a teller window. One of my co-workers was about twenty feet away from me near the door working at her desk. Another co-worker was directly behind me at the filing cabinets on the north side of the bank with her back turned.

On a chilly November morning at 9:05 a.m., the man who'd inevitably alter the path of my life as I knew it entered the bank. He walked slowly but directly toward my desk. He didn't look at the tellers behind the bullet resistant enclosure or the two other employees on the bank platform with me. I had the feeling he knew I was the Branch Manager, and had some important business to discuss with me. As it turned out, I was right.

I didn't recognize him as one of my customers and thought he wanted to open a new account. My experience taught me how to size up people who entered the branch as a customer, prospect, or potential security threat. At first look, he fit the profile of a businessman looking for a new banker. He dressed well and wore dark slacks, a button down shirt and a tan overcoat. He looked to be about forty years old, six feet tall and one hundred eighty pounds. He had a striking olive complexion with dark hair and eyes. He still didn't seem like a threat until he revealed his true motivation.

I placed the new account documents I was working on in my top desk drawer, and as he approached I stood up to greet him "Good morning." As he drew closer I could see the determined look on his face, like a man with a mission. Strangely, he responded to my greeting with complete silence. He then stretched out his left arm and handed me a 4 by 6 inch index card with a printed handwritten note. By now, his hand was trembling furiously and I knew he wasn't there to open an account.

This is the actual blood stained hold-up note, written by the Olive Skinned Man who sent me to Heaven.

(Front side)

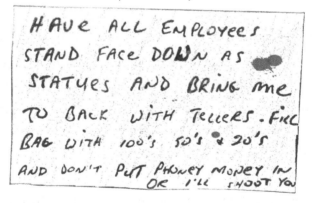

(Back side)

In nearly ten years of working in retail banking, this was the first and only holdup note I was ever handed. Through my experience, I've seen many different hold-up notes, but this was the most unusual I'd ever seen. It probably took me 20 seconds to read carefully, which is a long time considering the bank robber is in a hurry. This note was far more detailed, descriptive, and neater than usual. Most robbery notes don't include adjectives like "statues" and usually say to include only large bills rather than listing "100's, 50's & 20's". Perhaps this was his first bank robbery. But if so, then how would he know to make sure we didn't also include the bait money or phony money? Maybe this wasn't his first bank robbery, or maybe he once worked in a bank. Also, why would a bank robber list all the guns he brought to the robbery?

After I read the note front and back, I looked up at his face to see the expression in his eyes. The dread horror and carnal blood lust gleamed in his eyes like a neon sign at night. Terror consumed me as his intent was clear. There was no doubt he was angry and wanted to kill us the first chance he got. He knew I was the Manager but he wanted me to understand that he was now the Guy in Charge. Still, I don't know why he chose not to speak.

My concern was the safety of all the employees, especially those on the bank floor who were exposed to potential gunfire. I watched intently as his right hand sank into his right side overcoat pocket. It felt like time itself slowed down as he gradually revealed his Uzi machine gun. He slid out the Uzi three quarters of the way, enough for a good look. I remember thinking I had to stay calm and do whatever he wanted, or we could all die.

This potentially devastating weapon was his key psychological elicitor of fear. It could fire 20 bullets in only a few seconds, and cut a person in half. He showed it to me for five seconds before pushing the Uzi back into his pocket. From my years as a sportsman and hunter, I knew what the metal of a real gun looked like. I also knew for sure that what he had in his right side overcoat pocket was a fake Uzi made of plastic. The color was wrong and it was shiny, like plastic. Altogether, it wasn't a bad fake. The way he presented it plus the threatening note would've probably fooled many, but it was still a fake. This would explain why he didn't remove the gun from his pocket and reveal the orange plastic tip that most imitation guns have. Yet, I still knew by his bloodcurdling visage and his threatening note that he wanted to kill us.

After holstering his weapon, the Olive Skinned Man looked at me with an evil confidence to reinforce his dominance. The reaction in my facial expression however, wasn't what he was expecting. I didn't say a word, but he could clearly see that my expression gave away the undeniable. Now we both knew his Uzi was a plastic toy. I honestly couldn't help it, it was pure reaction. My eyes and facial twist gave me away for a split second. I knew he'd surely kill us all if I didn't give him the money, so I read the note once more to ensure I did exactly what he wanted.

As my eyes shifted from the note, back to his face, I saw a bead of sweat forming on his right cheek. Then he reached into his left side overcoat pocket and revealed the true weapon of our misfortune. The blued gunmetal briefly shimmered a reflection of light from its two and a half inch long barrel. It was a small but deadly weapon which I quickly recognized as a Jennings .22-LR caliber semi-automatic handgun. I'd seen this gun before and knew it could fire six bullets from its single stack magazine contained within the grip. I could see its distinctive vertical grooves on the action just behind the barrel. I knew this wasn't a toy; it was clearly the real deal.

The Jennings was now pointed directly at me, and I could see he was preparing to use it. My heart was pounding so hard that I could feel its vibrations straight through to my sweaty finger tips, which were still grasping the threatening note.

Standing there with his evil expression and his instrument of death pointed at me, I knew that we were all in grave danger.

A .22 caliber bullet is small, compared with a .38 or a .45 caliber. It has less mass and stopping force, but from a shooter's perspective it has its advantages. From a shooter's perspective, the .22 caliber is a deadly and forgiving bullet when fired into a warm body. A .22 caliber bullet fired from a pistol has a subsonic velocity, between 750-1000 feet per second, depending on the barrel length. The shorter the gun barrel, the slower the muzzle velocity. The bullet isn't in the barrel long enough to allow the gas from the powder burn inside the cartridge to accelerate it. Most .22 LR rounds will stay subsonic if fired from a barrel less than 4 inches long. This makes the .22 LR slower than the .38 or .45 calibers, which have a bigger powder charge, more projectile mass, and much greater stopping power.

Because of its slow velocity, the .22 LR fired from a handgun will usually not create an exit wound. After penetrating the flesh, the bullets deflect off tissue and bone, causing many small, hard-to-find wound channels. Shots that miss vital organs with their initial strike still have a good chance of eventually hitting a vital organ. That's why a .22 caliber is a forgiving round from a shooter's perspective. In the end, they create deadly wounds, cause massive internal bleeding, and usually result in death.

This flashed in my mind in seconds, but it felt like an eternity, as he continued to brandish his instrument of death. Angry and frustrated, the Olive Skinned Man boiled over, past the point of no return, but I wasn't sure why. I hadn't overtly challenged him or refused to comply with his demands. I would've done anything he wanted to protect my staff, including gift wrapping all the cash in a box.

After reflecting, I now believe he couldn't contain the ridicule he felt when he noticed that I recognized his Uzi as a plastic replica. I must've tested his patience during the two long periods it took me to read his instruction manual, I mean holdup note. So anguished, he decided his plan wasn't going the way he wanted or perhaps it was taking far too long. He didn't get any money that day, but I believe money wasn't the only thing he was after. Then he raised his weapon and decided the robbery was over.

I recall how he held the gun with confidence, as if it wasn't the first time he used it. He slowly removed his finger from outside the trigger guard and placed it onto the trigger. From across my desk I was helpless to defend myself, as he fired his weapon repeatedly. He fired at me first, as two bullets penetrated easily through my flesh. The first shot hit my right forearm and traveled up my arm. The second bullet tore through my torso just below the rib cage. It deflected inside me several times causing severe internal injuries.

I'll never forget how loud the shots rang out inside the bank walls. Without hesitation he redirected his death wish toward the Teller Manager, who was still standing several feet behind me at the filing cabinets. The gun exploded with all his fury as he fired the third and fourth shots at her, striking her on the side of the abdomen. This brutal gunman then spun around and headed for the exit, but not before he continued his rampage. Then he squeezed off two more rounds into the Customer Service Rep., who was still at her desk. The fifth shot struck her in her upper arm. Instinctively, she raised her hand out in front of herself in an attempt to protect her vital areas. When the sixth and final shot exploded out of the barrel, it tore directly into her hand, possibly saving her life.

By the time the shooter made it to the front door, I'd already reached under my desk and pulled the silent alarm. I vividly remember the sharp smell of gunpowder in the air and feeling my own hot blood flowing down my body and staining my pure white shirt. Still, my only concern was for my co-workers.

I turned around and bent down to comfort one worker who was lying on the floor, bleeding and screaming. I told her not move and that help was on the way. I remember standing up and walking the twenty or so feet to the Customer Service desk near the front door to help her. Despite her injuries, she remained calm and coherent. I remember her telling me in a calming tone of voice to stop walking around and to lie on the floor. She knew by my red soaked shirt that I was bleeding profusely and that walking around was making it worse. The room was thick with gun smoke and screams of the innocent. As I lie down to die on the bank floor, I could hear the constant ringing of a single telephone left unanswered.

The Most Glorious Place

I knew that I'd died when my spirit separated from my lifeless physical body and was hovering above it. As my spirit lingered in the still gun smoke filled room, I saw a co-worker struggling to open the double bank doors, to get help from anyone on the busy roadway. Then it began with a gentle touch on my right shoulder, and in front of me appeared a radiant woman who told me she was Our Lady of Mercy. Her touch alone transmitted intense feelings of complete peace and perfect love. She told me not to worry and guided me out of the bank, to the place I knew could only be Heaven.

In Heaven, I found myself standing in a vast expanse surrounded by beaming light which shown through a fine haze. The air was warm on my face and a pleasant aroma enveloped the entire space. I was still wearing in the same black pinstripe suit, red silk tie and white shirt from earlier that day. Yet, there was no longer blood on my white shirt and I felt no pain. I was no longer shot, my body was whole and I felt completely at ease in this extraordinary place. Everything around me was pure white and silence abound. As the fine haze dissipated, I stood before Our Lady of Mercy in the Most Glorious Place. Her face was picturesque with soft features and deep brown eyes. She wore long flowing pale clothes and she spoke in the sweetest tone I could ever imagine.

She raised her hands slightly above her waist and close together. Our Lady held in her hands a radiant ball of white light, and I could feel its warmth on my face. She extended her arms toward me and offered me this incredible gift. I raised my arms outward and accepted Her gift. When I did, She spoke these tender words: *"This is the Light of my Son Jesus, use it well. Today you will live again, for you have much to do."*

She didn't tell me what I had to do or how to do it, only that it was divine. As I received this most profound pronouncement from Our Lady of Mercy, I felt a tidal wave of warmth cascading through me. The Light was hot but it didn't burn me. The Light covered my whole body from head to toe and then filled me up inside like a sponge absorbing water. The only word to describe how I felt at that moment is blessed. I asked Our Lady how I'd know what to do with this gift, but She only told me to keep listening for the signs. Our Lady said *"I will always be with you to guide you, but this is not your time."* I asked Her to please let me stay with Her in Heaven but She replied *"You have much to do."*

I've been fortunate to experience great joy in my life, but none of it compared with the pure happiness I felt in Heaven. In Heaven, powerful feelings of perfect love and peace enveloped me. This Most Glorious Place healed me of every physical and emotional injury I ever had. My mind was clear and content, and devoid of all the petty issues that we typically worry about. Heaven is the greatest place in the universe and I never wanted to leave there.

Returning from Heaven, I saw myself lying motionless on the bank floor. Hovering in the air above my body, I watched the paramedics work on me. I heard them saying I didn't have any blood pressure or heart beat. They put what looked like a large black rubber cuff over my legs and inflated it with air. I later learned that this device squeezed the little blood I had left from my legs up to my vital organs. They were working furiously to bring me back to life. The paramedics had already cut away my suit jacket, shirt and pants to unveil the multiple gunshot wounds.

I felt my floating spirit drawn back into my physically broken body, and I'll never forget the moment when my body came back to life. It was an extreme and violent sensation. It felt like an explosion inside me, when my heart started to beat again, for the second time. My first breath was like a hurricane, filling up my lungs into my chest. I was alive once more, just as Our Lady of Mercy promised. I remember hearing one of the emergency medical technicians say, "It's a miracle." While I knew my body was torn to shreds, I also knew something no one else knew; I was going to live. I remember not being afraid. In fact, a peaceful strength enveloped me from the experience I had just a moment ago.

I desperately tried to see how my co-workers were, but I couldn't move. I asked the paramedic if they were alive and he told me they were. I knew the consequence of the deadly .22 caliber round that also hit them, and knew their lives were tentative at best. I could only pray that they received the same mercy that I did.

I overheard the other paramedic say I was stable and to prepare me for transport to the hospital. They skillfully placed me on the gurney and wheeled me out of the bank through the same set of double doors that I was paralyzed to open only ninety minutes before. At that moment, I understood the meaning of the warning the angels tried to convey that morning.

Before they placed me in the ambulance I told the paramedic my parent's phone number and asked him to call them and tell them that I was okay. He told me I shouldn't even be able to speak and asked me if I knew that I had just been shot. I remember the frigid air that morning and how cold it was when they took me out of the bank. I remember seeing so many red flashing lights from dozens of ambulance and police cars. The paramedics opened the back doors of the ambulance and wheeled me inside. As I lie motionless, I saw the light on the ceiling of the transport above my head. They locked the gurney in place and a paramedic told the driver we were ready to move.

I heard the driver turn the key to start the engine, but all I heard was a clicking sound of a dead battery. Looking up to ceiling of the van, I saw the light above my head dim to blackness. I saw the paramedic's face struck with momentary panic, and as he looked at me I said jokingly, *"This is going to ruin my whole day."* He responded, *"Do you realize that you were just shot and died, how are you joking"*? I just smiled and said "*You probably wouldn't believe me if I told you*".

They quickly removed me and transferred me to another ambulance. I was awake the whole time during the one and a half mile ride to Winthrop Hospital, in nearby Mineola. They took me out of the ambulance and wheeled my bloody body into the emergency room. A Trauma team was waiting to prepare me for the most arduous 77 days of my life. A wave of cold swept over my whole body as I began to shiver uncontrollably. One of the nurses gently held my hand and told me that I was going into shock.

Just before the doctors put me under with an injection, a Catholic priest from the hospital presented himself and gave me Last Rites. I could tell by his age that he'd performed this Rite many times before. The feeling I had by his facial expression was that I'd probably not survive. He anointed my forehead with oil in the sign of the cross and said "By the power of the Holy Spirit, I forgive you of all your sins, past and present." He explained that now my soul would be free to join God in Heaven. When he finished, he asked me if I wanted to say anything. I said, "Thank you for your prayer, but an angel of mercy told me that I will live today." I'll never forget his expression of puzzlement as I became drowsy from the anesthesia.

So on this cold November morning, I died and went to the Most Glorious Place. There, I met an Angel of Mercy who gave me a gift and a mysterious mission, and sent me back to the living. The last twenty three years of my life have been both arduous and prolific. I believe I was meant to die on that very specific 333rd day of the year. I believe that nothing as wondrous as a gift from God comes without great significance or sacrifice. What do you believe?

77 *Days*

The next 77 days in the Surgical Intensive Care Unit would prove to be the longest and most grueling of my entire life. Each day, when I thought the pain couldn't get any worse, it did. Each one was just like the one before it. The hospital had each minute of my life planned out and I felt like I couldn't make a single decision. I knew all my doctors and nurses were working hard each day and night to keep me alive. I also know the importance of all the machines and medical procedures that sustained my life. And I knew that I was a patient in their care.

But to me it all felt like a horrendous torture system designed to control my reality. I know it wasn't their fault, and I know they were all doing their job, but to me it was like prison. I couldn't move out of my bed. I couldn't urinate or move my bowels on my own. For 76 days, I couldn't eat or drink anything, and I couldn't shower. When I could get a moment of rest out of sheer exhaustion, a nurse would inevitably wake me to stick a needle in my arm or perform one of a dozen other procedures.

I remember slowly waking up from the anesthesia after the first ten hour surgery, and for ten seconds or so, blissfully not recalling the shooting or where I was. Then, like a dump truck unloading a ton of bricks right on top of me, it hit me. A quick flashback in my mind accompanied by the horrendous pain brought me back to this tragic reality. With my eyes still shut, I heard one familiar voice giving orders to all the nurses in the room. It was my wonderful friend Jenmarie Lettiere Byrnes. I'll never forget thinking to myself and chuckling, okay I'm definitely alive. Jenmarie had a tone about her, and I knew that if she was there, I was going to be okay. She wasn't going to let anything get between her and my life.

Growing up in Farmingdale N.Y., we lived across the street from the Lettiere family. I remembered that Jenmarie was a registered nurse but I didn't know that she worked at Winthrop Hospital. I later learned that Jenmarie didn't work at that hospital at all, but when she found out that I was in trouble, she simply dropped everything to come to my aid. She informed her boss that she had to go to help her friend and didn't know when she'd be back. Jenmarie put her own life on hold to save mine. She was ordering the nurses around in a hospital where she didn't even work. Wow, I thought. Listening to Jenmarie's voice and her instinctive desire to help me, when her own job might have been at risk, gave me strength and courage. I'll always remember her love and compassion and I'll pass it on to others who need help more than I do.

God knew I was going to need a fair amount of strength and courage in the months and years to come. Jenmarie eventually returned to work but constantly came to see me for the next 77 days at my new home. After twenty three years, Jenmarie continues to be a great friend and one of my personal heroes.

My parents and two brothers, Tom and Pete, were also by my side and I felt their hands touching me and whispering in my ears that they loved me. As the anesthesia wore off and I opened my eyes, I became aware of my surroundings. I soon realized the network of wires and tubes which were connected to my body. There was an intravenous line in my right arm providing me with various medicines. The nurses wrapped a blood pressure cuff around my left arm which automatically registered every thirty minutes. Protruding from the left side of my chest cavity was a large tube draining fluid from inside my chest cavity into a bag attached to the side of the bed. Another uncomfortable tube called a catheter fed into my urethra and drained the urine into yet another bag attached to my bedside. Then, a nasogastric tube or NG tube fed through my nasal passage and into my stomach. A nasogastric tube can be used to either provide nutrition directly into the stomach or to suction its contents. In my case, its purpose was to suction the contents of my stomach.

A machine with six multicolored wires attached to my chest constantly recorded my heart function. At the tip of my left index finger was a monitor that connected to a machine which measured my blood oxygen level. The doctors fed me oxygen through either an oxygen mask or a nasal cannula, which are thin tubes that enter ½ an inch into each nostril. As long as my blood oxygen level remained high enough, I could remain with either of these. But when my blood oxygen level dropped too low because my lungs weren't processing enough oxygen, the doctors connected me to a medical ventilator, or vent for short, which helped me to breathe. The ventilator tube inserted through my mouth and into my windpipe. Besides preventing me from speaking, you can imagine how uncomfortable a tube down my throat felt. What's more, the loud and incessant reverberation of the forced air traveling through the accordion shaped pump was like an acoustic torture.

It appeared I was in stable condition and with Mom and Dad by my bedside, we settled in for a long night. At 3:30 a.m., the doctors came into my room in a hurry to tell us they had to perform another emergency surgery. One of the bullets tore through my left kidney and the doctors tried to save it during the first surgery. They told us I was bleeding internally from my kidney and that they had to operate again. As the doctors prepared me for another surgery, a priest came in and performed the Last Rites for the second time.

The doctors told my parents in confidence that my life was in grave jeopardy. They immediately called Pete and Tom to tell them to come back to hospital because I might not make it. When I woke up from the second round of surgeries, I learned that they had to remove my spleen, left kidney, and part of my pancreas. They also told me the bullet came dangerously close to hitting my aorta, the body's main artery. They also told me I was lucky to be alive, but I knew that the bullet that didn't kill me was guided by the hand of Our Lady of Mercy.

There are subtle differences between good friends and great friends, yet these distinctions create brotherhoods that last a lifetime. My eyes were weary and closed, but one morning I heard the voice of a friend from High School. He moved away years ago, but we'd touch base from time to time. Even from the hallway, I was sure by his distinctive tone, that it was Mike Doner. He dropped everything, got on a plane and flew from Seattle, Washington to help me stay alive. When he came into my room and put his hand on my arm, I wept in the knowledge that he was silently giving me his strength. We were already very good friends, in spite of the distance between us, but on that day we became nothing less than Brothers. To Maria and me, he's family, as well to our children, he's Uncle Mike.

On the third day my breathing improved and I temporarily came off the respirator. With my whole family at my side, I insisted on getting out of bed and walking down the hall. I wanted to beat this and I knew the longer I stayed in that hospital bed, the longer it would take me to get out. Everyone thought it was a bad idea. Besides, they'd need a team of nurses just to hold me up and roll all the equipment down the hall. The doctors reluctantly agreed to allow me to try. I knew trying was never an option, the only option was doing.

Moving my body in any position was agonizing. You can only imagine how standing on my own two feet and walking was like. Of course, this was only the beginning of my pain. The only things holding my core abdominal muscles together were thread and staples. Each time I moved an arm or a leg in any direction, I became overwhelmed with agony. For a moment, I questioned my own actions, but then remembered the intense feelings of strength and comfort I felt when Our Lady of Mercy offered me the Light of Christ.

Recharged with the power of the Holy Spirit, I struggled to my feet and made it twelve steps down the hallway, just past the nurses' station, and then twelve steps back. I counted each one out loud for everyone to hear. In 1985 I ran a twenty six mile marathon with injured knees. I thought I knew what pain was until I walked those twenty four steps. This was the only time I could get out of bed and walk for many weeks but the Light of Christ continued to feed me with comfort and strength.

I realized the pain was here to stay. It had moved in like a deadbeat tenant. It drained my ice box but gave nothing in return. Like a frigid winter's blanket of snow, it would cover me up for many months to come. As each new day passed, my body became weaker and weaker, but my hatred for the Olive Skinned Man grew even more intense.

On one particular day, a mysterious stranger walked slowly into my room. As he stood at the foot of my bed shaking his head from side the side, I wondered who he was and what he wanted. He didn't dress like a doctor or a nurse and he didn't act like one either. He just stood there shaking his head back and forth. I thought he was the bearer of more bad news, but it wasn't anything like that.

At the time, I was 27 years old and this man looked slightly older than me, so I'd say he was about 33. As he moved closer to me, I noticed that he was slim, his hair was long and brown and his eyes were dark and deep. It felt like one of those moments when you just know something important is about to happen. The man walked to the right side of my bed and leaned over, peering directly into my eyes. People don't normally look at you the way that he looked at me. He definitely had my attention as he began to speak. He said "You're not supposed to be here. You were chosen for a purpose, and you must find out what it is." Temporarily stunned by his words, I never even had a chance to ask his name. After delivering his message, he turned around and walked out of my room, making a right into the busy hallway.

I immediately grabbed the nurses' call button tied onto the bedrail and pressed it repeatedly. When she arrived I asked her who the thin man with long brown hair was. She said he didn't resemble anyone that she'd ever seen in the hospital, and that he certainly didn't work on this floor. Out of concern for my safety and well being, she asked me if he bothered me. I thanked her and told her that it was nothing but I knew better. I knew that my visit from the slim man with long brown hair was most definitely something.

Over these many years, I've thought about the identity of the slim man with long brown hair. If he was a doctor or a nurse, he would've said so or least spoken about my medical condition, but he didn't. Also, most people aren't satisfied with talking only about you without inserting how your story relates to them, or how they have a friend who went through a similar situation. Inevitably, they always have to one-up your story with a tale of their own, but he didn't. Most people have the need to feel important, and want you to know who they are, invariably making sure that you know their name, but not him. Most people who start a conversation with a total stranger usually start with an ice breaker to ease the tension, but not the slim man with long brown hair. The slim man looked into my eyes and acted as though he knew me forever. He wasn't there to talk about himself, but only to deliver a powerful message. He wanted to make sure that I never forgot the significance of his visit, and I never have. So who was he?

I believe Angels of the Lord exist, and that they walk among us. I'm convinced the slim man was without a doubt one of God's Angels personified. But why me, why would God send an Angel incarnate to the S.I.C.U. in Mineola, N.Y. and deliver such a profound message? I'm not special; I'm just a regular guy. After two decades, I finally understand. God loves us all and I believe he is guiding us not just from Heaven, but with his own Angels here on earth. God has faith in us even when we don't have faith in ourselves, and even when we lose faith in Him. But when we express unconditional love and faith in God, He will most certainly reciprocate with unwavering commitment.

I realized that even during my darkest days, I never lost faith in God nor blamed Him for my pain and suffering. In fact, I thank God each day for allowing me to experience death, pain, anguish and forgiveness, because I now have a Survivor's Perspective that most people could never imagine. How could I possibly appreciate the joy of living that I can experience with each new day, without knowing dread, horror, and anguish? God's love and support is available to all of us and any of us, just take a step in the right direction, or simply leap. Think about this. As surely as there's a God, there's also a Devil, and so whom will you choose to believe in, whom will you choose to worship? In a world of light and darkness, if you turn away from the light, where does that leave you?

As the weeks passed I became wrought with terror, only imagining what grotesque horrors lay under my hospital gown as a result of the surgeries. But on one particular morning I mustered enough courage to lift the shroud, revealing the twenty three inch long incision littered with steel, suture, and latex. The first twelve inches which bisected my torso, stretched from below my belly button and ran straight up the middle of my body to the base of my chest. Then, the incision curved and ran another ten inches underneath my left pectoral muscle. But as a consolation prize, the trauma surgeon saved my belly button by cutting around it. It was beginning to look like a gruesome sight and that was only the beginning.

Dozens of surgical stainless steel staples fastened my torso together. To further secure my flesh from exposing my internal organs, fifteen retaining sutures covered the surgical wound. Each of the three inch long retaining sutures ran through thin latex tubes to protect my delicate skin. Of course, I understood the need for these drastic measures, but admittedly felt like a freak science experiment gone bad. As the days continued, I ran my fingers up and down those stainless steel surgical staples, retaining sutures, and tubes countless times. I thought that by touching them over and over, I might become less horrified of my new appendages, but I never did. I was so confused and had so many questions. Did I do something to deserve this fate? Why did God choose this path for me? How would I repay the Olive Skinned Man for his atrocities?

My determination to live was strong, yet the pain was formidable. Unaware the doctors were painting a grim picture to my parents of my chances for survival, I constantly challenged myself to recover quickly and leave the hospital. Mom and Dad were by my side every single day. On one particular afternoon, I was sitting up in bed talking to them. Suddenly, I couldn't breathe. I don't mean it was hard to breathe. I mean I was completely unable to breathe, like I was surrounded by water and wasn't getting any air at all. I started to panic, but remembered the universal sign for choking. So I clutched my hands to my throat and kept faith that I'd be saved. I remember my parents were screaming to call a doctor as I lost consciousness from lack of oxygen.

They later told me that my face turned the color of pale blue as the doctors rushed in with a crash cart, carrying medicine and equipment for use in emergency resuscitations. After the doctors revived me, I learned that I suffered congestive heart failure caused when my lungs filled up with fluid. My heart temporarily stopped beating, but they revived me just in time. I regained consciousness and realized my heart started beating again for the third time in my life. I still couldn't believe this was all happening to me, and I began to consider that He was testing me.

Days blurred with weeks as my decimation continued. My mind became tormented with the grim visage of evil, embodied by the face of the Olive Skinned Man. Each time I closed my eyes he was there, exploding his instrument of death. I don't think I slept at all in those 77 days, if it were not for the pain medication which temporarily rendered me unconscious. Through it all, Mom and Dad were my bastions of comfort and my faithful guardians. They gave me love and support and fought on my behalf with the hospital administration when they needed reminding that I was not one of their statistics. Terrified to close my eyes, my Dad asked the hospital staff to place a recliner chair in my room right next to my bed. So each night my Dad would fall asleep holding my hand to comfort me when the Olive Skinned Man returned in my nightmares.

My physical condition worsened as I developed an infection. When the bullet hit my pancreas, it caused pancreatic digestive enzymes to leach out. The enzymes normally used to break down food in the digestive tract escaped and they were digesting me from the inside out. Then on one particular day, the doctors discovered that the enzymes made a hole through my colon. They told me the colon was too weak to repair and that they would have to bypass it until it became stronger. Later that night they scheduled me for another surgery to bypass my colon and attach a colostomy bag to my abdomen. Now on top of it all, I had a gaping hole in my left side the size of a half dollar. It attached to a plastic pouch with a round seal over the top, and this was how I moved my bowels. The colostomy bag remained with me for another seven months until a surgeon successfully reversed it. Yet, each setback broke my will a little more but I continued to keep the faith that I knew Our Lady of Mercy had in me. But what was the point of it all?

After that my condition declined even further. A severe infection and a high fever set in. The doctors pumped round after round of broad spectrum antibiotics through my IV line but with no avail. I'll never forget when my doctor sat at my bedside and told me that I had sepsis. She said the infection spread into my blood and was now moving freely in my body. She explained how this blood infection triggered my body into producing a devastating and self-destructive immune response that could potentially lead to organ failure. I'd later learn from my doctor that the survival rate for septic infection is 35%, but because of my already weakened condition, my chances for survival were less than 20%. In any case, I was back on the critical list.

Then my doctor asked for my consent to administer the most powerful intravenous antibiotic they had in their arsenal of drugs. She said *"It's called Amphotericin, but we call it*

Amphoterrible because if it doesn't cure your infection, it will likely kill you." She explained that this drug's potential side effects might include; Anemia which is a decrease in the number of red blood cells, life threatening blood clots, acute fever, and kidney toxicity. Well, I already had an acute fever and only one kidney left, but no other options. I agreed to take the Amphotericin and prayed to Our Lady to hold my hand tightly.

After weeks of agonizing torturous pain, I became psychologically broken. I was so weak and I didn't have even an ounce of willpower left to sustain me. I remember the moment clearly. On one particular afternoon I was alone in my room. The orderly just left the room and I could smell the disinfectant on the freshly cleaned floor. I saw the nurses passing in the hallway outside the door. For them it was just another day at work, but for me it felt like the end.

I had nothing left and I didn't know what else to do, so I began to speak to God. Tears drenched my face and my voice cracked in and out of tones. Ruled by my pain I began to shout loudly, and I said *"God, the pain is too much and I can't take another minute of it. Why would you save me, only to torture me so? I don't care what the consequence is, just end my pain now!"* I sank into my bed, struggling even to catch my breath.

Suddenly, everything became silent. The bustling sounds of the nurses outside my room became barely audible. Even the beeping sounds of the machines from inside my room became scant. Mine was still the only heartbeat in the room, yet at that moment another physical voice resounded strongly from within the four walls. It was a strong, masculine voice and it was responding to my cry for relief. I heard the voice clearly as it said, *"If you want an end to all of your pain, simply let go of your will to live and you will be released. Give up and you will come Home. The choice is yours."*

I'll always remember that moment for as long as I live. The voice never used his name, and I didn't ask, but I knew that it must be God. I felt strangely composed to hear the voice of God come literally out of nowhere, and in a way it calmed me when He responded to my plea. At that instant, I knew if I gave up my fight to survive and unquestionably released my will to live, that I'd soon be back in Heaven, the Most Glorious Place. I thought for a second of the intense feelings of complete peace and perfect love I experienced when I met Our Lady of Mercy in Heaven. If I chose to return to Heaven, all my pain would melt away for eternity, and there was nothing more that I wanted than for my pain to end.

Then something remarkable happened. Instead of giving up, I responded to the Lord's offer in a most unexpected and remarkable fashion. When God spoke to me, He resurrected the fortitude of my will to live. It was like He injected me with the seed of His strength. I don't know exactly what it was, but I felt rejuvenated and more alive than ever. Despite my feeling of intense pain which still enveloped my body like a straitjacket, I shouted with passion, *"Thank you God, I can feel Your Light burning brightly inside me. I choose to live, even with the pain. With your strength, I can endure any pain this world can devise."* Within a day, my septic blood infection and high fever were gone, and I was still alive. The doctors told me the Amphotericin cured me, but I knew that I wouldn't be alive, if not for the Hand of God.

In case you're wondering, I never regretted my decision to choose living with pain over an opportunity of joining God and Our Lady of Mercy in the Most Glorious Place. I know that I'll not fear death when it finally comes to me, and I'll see Our Lady in Heaven once more. Please remember that although my experiences are special, I'm not. I'm an ordinary man, and you have the same opportunity for a relationship with our Lord as I do.

Some people consider faith to be a crutch, and they say it makes us weak and crippled, but I see it differently. *Faith isn't a crutch used by the frail to prevent them from falling over. Faith is our mighty staff which we wield as we walk through the valley of our personal shadow of death. It's true that we sometimes require our staff to lean on and provide us with strength and courage, but no more than those who lack faith and lean on the truly feeble power of money.* That day I learned that God had always been with me, I just didn't fully understand it until I opened my heart and invited Him in. God is also with all of you and all you have to do is open your heart to realize it. I know that God and Heaven are as real as you and I so believe it and be filled with the greatest power imaginable. *Take a leap of faith, because if you're not risking something, you're not truly living.*

By mid December of 1990, the Christmas Holiday was almost upon us. As the rest of the Christian world was preparing to celebrate the birth of Christ, I remained in a sterile hospital room hanging on to the edge of my life. My parents and brothers had no joy that holiday. They didn't hang a wreath on their front door, or set a Balsam Fir in their living room, as long as I couldn't be there to celebrate with them. But what I've learned, and what I need you to always remember is that where there's a will, there's a way!

T'was the week before Christmas and all through the ward, all the bells and the pumps were blaring their fiord. The IV's were hung by the bedsides with care, in hopes that patients' health would soon be fair. The nurses settled in for a long busy day, as phlebotomists all practiced their curious way. When from out in the hallway there came such a fuss, the oohs and aahs made me perk up. The light from the crest of the freshly waxed floor, shown tinsel and angel all over the hall. When what to my baby blue eyes should appear, but a miniature tree held by my brother Pierre.

Pete walked into my room gleaming and carrying a miniature artificial Christmas tree, completely decorated with ornaments, lights and a little angel nestled on top. My brother Tom and my parents were right behind him, and all were shining brightly. As Pete set the tree by the window, Tom presented me with a large wooden crucifix which he placed at my bedside. If I couldn't come to Christmas at home, then they'd bring Christmas to me. And that's exactly what they did. So despite our obvious tragedy, we shared Christmas together as if nothing had changed. My family helped me to remember that home is where the heart is, even if you're living in a hospital. Then, as if it couldn't get any better, Pete handed me a poem he wrote especially for me. I still cry when I read it even after all these years.

I Sit and Pray

Day by day I sit and pray,
That soon the sun will shine.

And happiness will come his way,
Hoping the future will turn for the better and
Waiting for the day when a smile breaks through.

When the clouds of sorrow are overcome,
By untouchable bright skies of blue.

Like springtime,
When animal and nature are as one.

The mountains in autumn,
The frigid pure streams,
So powerful as they run.

Placid and silent,
The snow blankets the earth.

The warm ocean waves,
Pounding the Sandy shores,
As gulls are heard above.

For now I sit and pray,
That happiness will come his way.

By: Peter Palasciano

January came, and brought more monotony and struggle. Still hooked up to machines, tubes, and catheters, it felt like my recovery was nowhere in sight. It became increasingly difficult to breathe and my doctors suspected an infection had spread around my right lung. Their effort to drain the infection by inserting a chest tube was unsuccessful, so they scheduled me for a surgery called a thoracotomy. The doctor described the surgery as being extremely traumatic but completely necessary. In my weakened state, my parents opted for a surgical second opinion. It was subsequently decided that the surgery would be postponed for two weeks until I was physically strong enough to survive it. Later that month I underwent the procedure and lost a small part of my right lung.

It was now mid-February and I thought I might never escape from my prison. One night, the Chief of Surgery came into my room and asked me how I was feeling, I responded, "Not so good." But what he said next took me completely by surprise. After examining me, he looked straight at me and asked, "Would you like to go home?" I replied, "Sure I would, when I'm well enough." He responded, "I believe you're well enough right now. Besides, you'll recover a lot quicker at home than you will in a hospital." I said, "Are you sure, I still feel pretty sick?" His response was certain, "Rob, you don't need to be in a hospital to get better." Then he told me that he arranged for my release the following morning and that I should make plans to go home. He also said I could eat real food again for the first time in 76 days, and to expect a meal tray of soft food from the kitchen for dinner.

I immediately jumped on the phone and called my folks to tell them the great news. They were as astonished as I to hear the news. I couldn't wait to feel the texture of real food again. They hurried over, but not before stopping for some delicious takeout at Vincent's Clam Bar in Carle Place, one of my favorite Italian Restaurants. I'll never forget the moment they walked into my room. For the first time in 76 days, there were smiles all around. What's more, Mom and Dad presented me with the most memorable meal of my entire life. I was already salivating from the distinctive wafting scent of great Italian food. I opened the lid with great anticipation to reveal several regal manicottis, flawlessly covered in red sauce. I knew then, for the first time the end was in sight.

On Thursday February 14, 1991 after 77 grueling days, I finally left the hospital and was going home. That day proved to be a milestone, yet my journey was only beginning. I rose from the bed, sat in a wheel chair and never looked back. My whole family joined me, with Dick Crowley and Ed O'Donnell. I felt so excited at the prospect of breathing in fresh air and feeling the sun on my face. The doors opened, I took my first breath and thanked Mother Mary for having faith in me. Then Dick and Ed presented me with 77 red, white, and blue balloons, one for each day I spent in the hospital.

The Bank's Long Island Headquarters was less than a mile from Winthrop Hospital. Ed told me that my friends there were waiting for me to give them the signal that I was out. All I had to do was release the 77 balloons into the air. It was an incredible plan and as I released them, the feeling was nothing less than cathartic. Then my Dad pulled up in his yellow 1973 GMC motor home, which we affectionately called our Yellow Submarine. We boarded and drove to their house in Farmingdale to celebrate our victory over this battle. At the time, I didn't realize the war would continue for more than twenty years.

It's important to understand how these 77 days changed my life. The most profound change which occurred within me was my understanding of the difference between my belief in God and my faith in God. I've always believed in God and felt that He was with me, but my experiences during these 77 days solidified my belief into an unwavering faith. So what's the difference? I used to live my life in the knowledge that He existed and was around me. I spoke to Him as many of you do, and hoped that He heard me. When I had success, I even thanked Him. I thought that my belief would somehow benefit me. But what was God getting in return? What was I doing to show my belief in Him?

For me, the difference between belief and faith is the action I take to show God that I love him. Faith is showing other people the love God has for them. *Having faith in God means extending yourself into uncharted waters, exposing your heart and soul so others may benefit, even when it's inconvenient. Faith is an unwavering trust, which gives us the power to overcome any obstacle at any time.*

Through each of the 77 days, I always had faith that God was with me, giving me the power to endure and survive. I remembered my experience in Heaven with Our Lady of Mercy. I remembered the feeling of the powerful ball of light that She gave me as it coursed through my spirit, and when she told me that I would live once more. I believe God has faith in me because I have faith in Him. I believe God saved me because He believes that I am worth saving. I don't blame God for allowing this atrocity to happen to me, and I don't believe that He was punishing me. Please don't blame God for the poisonous acts of those people who've hurt you, and the ones you love. God wants us to grow from these experiences. Perhaps it's His way of testing us. *Perhaps true faith can only be born from the ashes of our own personal hell.* If so, how will you respond?

Chapter Three
THE BANK'S RESPONSE

Throughout our lives we've often heard how dire the world is to live in because of the evil that lurks in the hearts of mankind. We're taught not to trust those around us for fear of injury. What's more, it's instilled in us that all large corporations are calculating and heartless. While it's undoubtedly true that evil exists around us, it's paramount to understand that, given the opportunity, the goodness of mankind will always rise to the occasion and squelch the evil. During the worst days of my life, the actions and prayers of so many at The Bank of New York® would surely serve as a testament to the goodness we've all inherited from God.

When I became hospitalized from the gunshot wounds, The Bank responded unfalteringly and with great generosity. Dick Crowley was a Senior Vice President in charge of all retail branch banking for Long Island. Ed O'Donnell was a Vice President and my District Manager. According to the account of my parents, Dick Crowley called them at home on the morning of November 29th and asked them to meet him at Winthrop Hospital in Mineola. Dick knew that if my Mom and Dad were aware of what happened, they'd panic as they drove to the hospital. So to avoid them from becoming injured in a car accident, he calmly told them that I had a small car accident and had broken my arm. He told them I was fine and was at Winthrop Hospital, where he would meet them in the emergency room.

My brother Pete was visiting Mom and Dad that morning at their home, so he drove them to the hospital. They passed through several police roadblocks which caused their delay to the hospital. They never realized the roadblocks were in place to catch the man who'd just shot three innocent people, one of them their own son. When they finally arrived Pete dropped them off at the door and then parked the car. Dick and Ed met my parents as they walked steadily through the doors into the emergency room.

When they introduced themselves as Tom and Gerry Palasciano, Dick Crowley uttered the undeniable words that would alter the course of their lives, *"Rob has been shot in a bank robbery!"* His words struck them down with horror. Their pain was so great that the bullets may as well have torn through their own flesh. They collapsed in tears, gasping to catch their breath, but Dick and Ed were at their sides to provide them with strength and comfort. When Pete walked in shortly after and saw them collapsed and in tears, he knew that it wasn't over a broken arm. He knew that tragedy struck. The doctors told my family that my chances for survival were minimal, due to the extent of my injuries. Soon after, my brother Tom joined them, but all they could do was feel helpless.

During this unforgiving and dark crisis facing my family, a beacon of hope shined strongly through. My family wouldn't be alone. Both Dick Crowley and Ed O'Donnell posted a constant vigil and stayed with my family in the hospital waiting room for days and nights on end. Dick and Ed literally camped out with my family in the hospital, praying and waiting for any glimmer of hope. My parents told me that Dick Crowley took his rosary beads out of his pocket and prayed almost continuously, asking God to spare my life. Ed O'Donnell brought me his most treasured and blessed rosary beads from Knock Ireland.

On a Thursday evening on August 21st 1879, Our Lady, St. Joseph and St. John the Evangelist appeared at the church at Knock, County Mayo, Ireland. There were fifteen witnesses to the apparition who watched and prayed for two hours in the pouring rain. Ed O'Donnell placed his precious rosary beads around my neck to protect me, where they would stay for 77 days.

What you must realize is that at the time, I'd only worked for The Bank for about five months, and barely knew Mr. Crowley and Mr. O'Donnell. I saw Mr. Crowley at monthly district meetings and met with Mr. O'Donnell once a week at the Branch Manager's Meetings. Neither Ed nor Dick knew me personally, yet they both shed their own work and family responsibilities to pray for my recovery alongside my own family.

We hail these two men, like angels sent directly from Our Lady of Mercy, as faithful and stalwart companions. Dick and Ed were present, praying with my family, for every single surgery regardless of the time of day. They didn't have to be there, providing my family with hope and support, but they chose to be there. In my monotony, the daily event that kept me upbeat and moving forward was my visit, without fail, from Ed O'Donnell. He didn't have to come to see me every single day for 77 days, but he came anyway and I'll never forget his kindness and laughter during the days of dread.

I cannot fully express the love and compassion they offered my family and I. These were men who I hardly knew, opened their hearts and souls so we could find kindness and hope in such a desperate time. I became good friends with them and often shared stories over a beer or at the annual Bank picnic. We should all take their example and remember to go out of our comfort zone to help one another, even if it inconveniences us. Sadly, Dick Crowley's time with us was cut short and I'll miss him dearly. Yet, the memory of his actions will live on. He is proof that incredible compassion exists in this world. We need to follow his example and help other people, even if it inconveniences us. It's easy to close our eyes to others in need and say that we don't have any time. Yet, the subtle rewards of our good deeds will continue for generations to come.

The first time I met Dick Crowley was in his office, located at 1401 Franklin Avenue in Garden City, NY. It was a warm spring day in 1990 and he was interviewing me for a job as a Branch Manager. Mr. Crowley sat there, distinguished and poised, as he reviewed my resume and asked me a series of questions. He noticed I spent time at several different financial management companies and banks. He pointed out his concern that I might only stay at The Bank for the experience until I moved on again. I'll always remember that particular moment when I said, "Mr. Crowley, I'll work hard for The Bank and I am looking to grow with a financial organization that I can finally call Home." Mr. Crowley hired me on the spot by saying "Welcome Home Rob." Little did I know the impact that his welcome would one day, come to have.

Mr. J. Carter Bacot was The Chairman of the Board of Directors for The Bank of New York® at the time. He was the top guy at The Bank and he had time for little else, yet he took a day to day interest in the well-being of both my parents and I. Mr. Richard Field served as a Senior Executive Vice President for The Bank's Retail Division and was a member of the Senior Policy Committee. Mr. Field's position was also especially demanding. Nonetheless, Messrs. Field, Bacot, and Crowley all made my family and I all feel as though we were their top priority.

From day one, there was a concern for my safety. They believed that because I could identify the unknown shooter, he might try to finish the job by slipping into the hospital and murdering me for good. In response to this potential threat, senior bank officials acted decisively with a three-pronged strategic plan. First, they directed hospital administration to list my admission under an assumed name, to protect my identity from the gunman. Second, they hired and paid for an armed guard service, which posted a bodyguard outside my hospital room door, 24/7 for a whole month. Third, The Bank posted a $25,000 cash reward for information leading to the arrest of the assailant and advertised it in all the major area newspapers.

The Bank of New York® spared no expense to ensure my comfort and that of my parents. The Bank's Senior Management instructed the hospital to place me in a private room during my stay, and indicated that they would pay for everything that wasn't covered by Workmen's Compensation. Even though my room was directly across from the nurse's station, The Bank arranged and paid for a private nursing service to help me during the day. The Bank offered to rent a suite for my parents at the five-star rated, Garden City Hotel, for as long as I was in the hospital. The Bank also offered to put at their disposal, a private car service, to take them each day from the hotel to the hospital and back. While this would provide my parents with comfort and convenience in their trying time, they graciously declined. They chose instead to drive themselves each day to the hospital from their home in Farmingdale. In total, The Bank spent several hundred thousand dollars of related medical expenses out of its own pocket, and they never asked me to pay back a penny.

The Bank continued to handle my situation with great generosity and latitude. The Bank also decided to continue to pay my full salary for as long as I couldn't return to work because of my physical and psychological injuries, even after I left the hospital. Just before Christmas of 1990, J. Carter Bacot himself made a special trip to visit with me in the hospital. Mr. Bacot sat by my bedside and we talked, one-on-one, for about forty minutes. His concern for me was overwhelming and genuine. He was generous with his time, and I told him so. I thanked him for all that he'd done to help my parents and me. He thanked me for all my hard work at The Bank and I told him that I was looking forward to coming back to work as soon as I could.

Mr. Bacot promised me that I didn't have to come back to work as a Branch Manager and that I could choose any bank division I wanted. He promised me that as long as I continued to support The Bank now and in the future that The Bank would always continue to support me when my injuries prevented me from working. He said, *"Rob, you have a job for life at The Bank."* He was sincere, and we shook hands on it. Just before he left, Mr. Bacot gave me two gifts. An official Bank of New York tie which I wore to several subsequent annual meetings, and a book of the history of The Bank of New York® which he inscribed for me.

Carter Bacot also wrote me a letter the day I came home. It said,

Dear Rob:

It's great news to hear that you have left the hospital and are feeling much better. I know it was a long and difficult siege and I admire your fortitude in getting through it. All of us have been thinking of you, and I plan to stop by and see you some time soon.

Best wishes.
Sincerely,
Carter

The Bank's Senior Management continued to assure me that I was a valued member of The Bank's family. On March 20th 1992, Mr. Field invited me to join him in the executive dining room in The Bank's Headquarters, located at One Wall Street. We talked about politics, the history of The Bank, and even a recent skiing adventure he had. Mr. Field made it clear to me that The Bank would always support me due to the events of 11/29/90. There was no doubt that The Bank of New York® was my Home away from Home.

In addition, The Bank offered to pay for the best plastic surgeons to erase the several feet of scars on my torso. While I appreciated their offer, I declined. I'd grown attached to my battle scars and felt that they would serve me well as a reminder of how physical challenges, no matter how enormous, can be overcome through our faith in God.

After I left the hospital on February 14th, I worked hard to regain my physical strength. At first, my limit was walking up a flight of stairs once or twice a day. After a few weeks I could walk a third of a mile around the block. Shortly after, I began to lift light weights. While my body was still weak and recuperating, my will to recover remained strong. I spent the next five months physically retraining my body with strength training and long-distance running.

My body responded quickly and in July of 1991 I asked Dick Crowley if I could return to work part-time, as I couldn't yet physically work an eight-hour day. He told me that he'd be glad to have me back, even part-time, until I could put in a full day. Dick made it clear to me that I didn't ever have to be a Branch Manager again and asked me what I wanted to do. I asked Dick to counsel me regarding the choices for my long-term career path with The Bank, which he gladly agreed to. I suggested that for the short-term, I could fill a role as an on-site Sales Coach for the Client Service Representatives who worked in the branches opening and servicing accounts.

I explained that while it sounded a little like sales training, that it was different. He said that we didn't currently have any program like it at The Bank. I agreed, and then shared with him the action plan which I'd created for the new program. Dick said he liked the idea and that I'd report directly to him. He gave me the flexibility to make my own hours and to carry out the program in as many Long Island Branches as possible. I worked in this new improvised position for eight months until I was strong enough to return to work full-time in March of 1992.

By now, Dick Crowley and I became close friends. He advised me to accept a position in the Bank's Credit Division as a Credit Analyst. He explained that my degree in Finance and Banking from Hofstra University suited me for the job. He told me that the Credit Division would provide me with a place to grow as a banker and offer me opportunities for upward mobility. I spent the next four weeks quietly behind a desk with reams of corporate financial statements and a calculator. I analyzed the financial strengths and weaknesses of commercial clients in need of financing. While I appreciated the opportunity that Dick offered to me, I was going mad from the silence and lack of communicating.

I'd always been in financial sales and needed to meet with clients face-to-face. I met with Dick and explained that I wasn't fitting into the new job in the Credit Division and asked him for something more suitable for me. A few days later Dick called me and asked if I'd like to join the Cash Management Division as a Sales Officer. I relished the opportunity, joined the Cash Management Division and became one of their top salespeople for twelve years straight.

Chapter Four
WISDOM AND PERSONAL REVELATION

How arrogant are we to believe we're in control of anything, much less our own destiny. All we can do is pray for God's divine guidance and follow the path Home.

December 2006

Who Am I, Lord?

Who am I, Lord? You've taught me so much in my life, and I thank you for all of it. I've always tried to find the lessons you meant for me, and to become the man you wanted me to be. I'm so sorry if I failed you, otherwise why would you continue to tear my mind from me? Your own Mother offered me your Light and instructed that I should use it well, and to that end I can feel your fire burning brightly within me.

Yet, I still don't know how to use it, and I fear I've failed you. But why my Lord, does my torment continue still? Who am I, Lord? How can I fulfill my promise to Our Lady of Mercy, if I'm only half a man? Who am I, Lord? Is *the pain and loss which I feel, completely necessary to carry out your work?*

I ask that you offer me the strength and courage to finish this work, as I know it's the reason I'm here. Please bless my family with your wisdom, as you have blessed me. Lord, I remember now who I am. I am your servant.

If you're like me, I know you were great at what you did but now you can't do that anymore. I understand how it's possible to recover superficially for many years from the effects of Trauma Induced Stress, only to have them return years later, but even more severely. In mid 1993, my nightmares of blood and death inexplicably loosened their grip on my mind. The feeling I had of constantly being on my guard, for fear that I was in danger also subsided and I no longer needed prescription drugs. However, I continued looking for the face of the Olive Skinned Man in crowds wherever I went, hoping to someday exact revenge. As well, my feelings of guilt and anger stayed with me for many years to come.

Before my relapse disabled me from working in August of 2004, I was a Vice President and a Cash Management Sales officer for The Bank of New York®, now The Bank of New York Mellon®. I managed hundreds of clients and was consistently top three in sales each year. And although my job was demanding, I was still able to maintain a happy and productive relationship with my gorgeous wife Maria and our three beautiful children, Adam, Jessica and Stephen. Then, on one particular day, it felt like the weight of the world came crashing down on top of me. Every unresolved emotion I harbored and locked tightly inside the vault which I created in my mind broke out and escaped. The resulting cataclysm crushed my constitution into a fine powder and withered my hopes and dreams for the future.

For us survivors, one of the difficulties coping with Trauma Induced Stress is that people looking at us can't tell we're suffering. It affects us on the inside, even though we appear well enough on the outside. When the reoccurrence knocked me down in 2004, I was physically in good shape, so based on outward appearances I looked normal. That's the quandary, you can't see it, and those looking at me couldn't understand.

Even when we explain how we feel, they can't believe we're psychologically and emotionally crippled. Of course they understand when our trauma first occurs, it's still fresh. For them, the difficulty arises after we've apparently appeared to recover from the emotional trauma for many years. They have difficulty understanding what's wrong with us because our initial trauma was so long ago.

The other challenge is that there's no bloody gash on our forehead. Our gash is inside our head, and it changes us in horrible ways. It lives inside of us, changing our personality and dramatically tampering with our thoughts and feelings. Eventually, our lives our driven by feelings of anger, terror, and guilt, and everyone expects us to make believe that it's all better because they say it's over. But in fact it's not over; rather it's only beginning. So for years we've lived with this unwelcomed guest until we find solace.

My path to recovery has been long and treacherous and continues still. But I've learned greatly from my experiences and I feel compelled to share these stories with you. I realize how your attacks of anxiety bring you to the brink of losing consciousness. I understand how the physical shaking of your hands is so dramatic that you can't even hold a cup without spilling it. I know they tell you that you're simply having an anxiety attack, and all you have to do to shake it is to take deep breaths. Of course, this is ridiculous.

I share your despair as your legs shudder and prevent you from standing up. I understand that before your relapse of Trauma Induced Stress, that you were emotionally well balanced. Like me, you could manage the complexities of family life, as well as a stressful job with no problem at all. It all seemed to work well despite what happened those many years before. Like me, you consider yourself to be a survivor and not a victim. Regardless, the reckless remnants of traumatic events rear their stagnant heads to wreak havoc directly upon you, the likes of which you've never experienced before. The good news is that you're not alone and there's a way out of the mire.

I understand how it feels to crumble under the strain of simple tasks like trying to make breakfast. Do your hands shake so much that cracking an egg into a frying pan without making a mess is a feat? Is holding a spatula and flipping it over without shuddering as you drop the egg directly on the stovetop a daily challenge? It is for me, and that's the easy stuff.

After my relapse of Trauma Induced Stress, my brain seemed to stop working. Trying to pay bills, write checks, and do simple math became impossible. What's more, I'd lost the ability to hold a pen and write anything legibly including my own name. Even the simple skill of tying a necktie seemed like a distant memory inside my mind. The knowledge was in my head but I couldn't get it out. My hands simply couldn't maneuver to perform simple activities that were second nature to me. I'd once been a fair piano player, but after my relapse I sounded like a neophyte. But it was even worse than that. I was no longer able to read the music in front of me. I could see the notes, but it didn't translate into anything. I felt broken, disconnected, and alone.

I recognize that you were the best at what you did before your trauma crushed the life you once had, and left you feeling like a feeble idiot. Of course, you're not a feeble idiot. I understand how your mind, which was once quick and sharp now feels slow and dull. I realize how you could manage ten separate projects all at once, and now you have difficulty focusing on a single task. I also know that you used to command language and the proper words would simply roll off your tongue in any conversation. Like me, now your brain feels slow and dull and it's a challenge and sometimes even embarrassing to hold a conversation. I know this because it's how I once felt. I can appreciate how all of these things combine to make you feel like you're all alone. Please recognize that you are not alone as we are many and we can help each other.

I understand that your constitution was once unshakable and even the greatest pressures couldn't throw you off your game. Yet, now the smallest derailment can ruin your whole day. It might come in the form of a sharp sound or an unexpected touch on the shoulder. It may also come from a strong odor, or the visual impact of a person or place. I understand how you feel and you are not alone. Doctors call this reaction a *startle response*, but that's just too simple a phrase to describe how we feel and respond when our particular button is pushed.

Clinically, a startle response is a reaction to an unexpected and surprising stimulus, like a sudden noise or an unexpected physical touch, smell or sight. It's categorized as a physiological reflex which can be treated with psychotropic medications. It sounds so simple and of course clinical. But for those of us suffering from the tangible effects of a startle response, there's nothing simple or clinical about it.

What's more, anti-anxiety medications don't always work, and can be mind altering and highly addictive. If fact sometimes their undiagnosed side effects can replicate the very symptoms they were designed to alleviate. This may result in higher and higher prescribed doses and worsening symptoms. That's exactly what happened to me when a doctor prescribed Xanax to manage the symptoms of my anxiety condition. I've been free from Xanax as well as any mind altering or addictive drug for many years now, and I am the better for it. Of course, only a qualified doctor should manage prescription medication. Also, you should never self-medicate or attempt to stop taking a medication without the advice of a qualified doctor. This is imperative, especially when the medication is addictive or mind altering.

My startle response is a very real and visceral event which momentarily causes me to lose focus on reality. Then, it drags me back to the instant when a gun exploded with a hail of fire so fierce that it nearly took my life and the lives of two coworkers. For me, quiet places are soothing until an unexpected noise shatters the silence and scares the hell out of me, especially if I'm alone in my home.

Unexpected rings of a doorbell or telephone are common culprits. Any one of dozens of innocuous objects may accidentally fall to the floor with a bang and do their worst on me. Although, there's one particular innocuous object that I dread above all others, and it's inescapable. Having raised three children, we've had our share of birthday parties, and with them the trimmings, including the dreaded latex party balloon. When you're a kid, all party balloons end with a bang, except for me it's an actual BANG! Yet, I refused to deny my kids the joy which comes from popping balloons. The worst part is that it was my job to blow them up, even after they exploded in my face. Man, do I love my kids!

After the trigger goes off, there's no stopping the process. I can hardly catch my breath as my legs buckle beneath me. My heart begins to pound so hard that I fear for my life. It feels like time slows down as I'm utterly helpless and moving to find the nearest safe place to hide. In the past, the dramatic effects of this triggered response lasted for hours and it took the aid of family and friends to help me realize that we were in fact not in mortal danger. While I still respond negatively from unexpected loud noises today, the extent of their effects is not so dramatic or long lasting. It's my hope that you too can find relief from these effects.

I believe our startle response is borne from the constant vigil that we portray. This state, also known as *hyper-vigilance*, is what causes us to be on guard 24/7. This constant state of high alert forces us to expect danger around every turn, as we're determined to protect ourselves and our families. But as you well know, we cannot sustain this level of hyper-vigilance without serious ramifications.

I know it's difficult for those not suffering from a life altering traumatic event to understand why we're sometimes terrified to leave our own homes, or be in a crowded restaurant. I understand that they cannot fathom how we've lost the ability to filter out the many other conversations in a room and focus on the one we're trying to have with another person. My hope is that this story will somehow help them to understand us better.

As a trauma survivor, I know you feel like someone turned up the volume and sensitivity in your ears by a factor of 100. I empathize how this forces you to retreat into solitude, where even the sound of a spoon touching your morning coffee cup sounds like someone beating a drum inside your head. During these days, my greatest ally was the silencing headset I used to deaden the sound of gunshots at the rifle range, just before hunting season. Of course, I haven't hunted in over twenty years. Before I met the Olive Skinned Man, busy restaurants, wedding receptions and morning coffee used to be a cinch. But as these symptoms lapsed and relapsed, these activities became impossible to manage.

Like me, I know you feel you were once normal and great at everything, but not so much anymore. I understand you feel like you were once smart, mentally strong, and emotionally balanced. What you may not realize is, there's a way out of our seemingly endless maze of horror. The reason I'm compelled to write this book is to enlighten you and help you understand that you can defeat your monster, and overtime reshape it into your greatest strength. With the proper tools, you can re-shape your life with your family. You will improve. Your sharp mind will return, your emotions will stabilize and you'll become even better than you were before. So please follow me, because I just might know what you're feeling even better than you understand it yourself. I believe it all starts with a little faith; from there the possibilities are endless.

Look, I know you have your doubts. I know you're asking yourself how it's possible to feel better, and once again feel smart, emotionally stable, and just plain happy. I know all this because for many years I asked myself the same questions. While I can't offer you a magic potion, I can offer you a reassurance that there's a better way to live. It's been more than twenty three years since the Olive Skinned Man shot me. My physical recovery has taken years but my mental recovery has been in and out of shades from heaven to hell for more than two decades. I believe I've found some of the answers to the questions we have in common.

I've always wondered why Our Lady of Mercy would spare my mortal life and return me from that Most Glorious Place in Heaven, only to inflict me with suffering. So every morning I pray to God and Our Lady of Mercy and thank them for each new and glorious day. And each night before bed I pray and ask them to end my torture. But on one particular day, I had an eye-opening thought. What if I was asking God for something He wasn't prepared to offer me? What if, instead of asking Him to heal my suffering, I asked the Lord for something I could use to heal myself?

I asked Our Lady of Mercy for Her guidance, and one day it came to me. The obstacle I faced, the thing I needed most to help me get through these tough times and move on with my life, was wisdom. So I began to pray, asking Jesus and Mother Mary to grant me the gift of wisdom, for I believed that through understanding, I could begin to heal. As weeks passed, I continued to pray for the gift of understanding, and I thought about the issues which troubled me most.

Chapter Five

GUILT, VENGEANCE & THE PATH TO FORGIVENESS

March 2005

Dear God,

The pain and anger are strong within me. They've taken on a life of their own, and they want to come out and gain revenge against the one who's damaged me. But if my demons cannot gain vengeance on the Olive Skinned Man, then they're content enough to inflict pain on the ones that I love. I battle these demons relentlessly, but as each day passes I become weaker and unable to hold them at bay. My attempts to contain them in a locked compartment within my mind have been futile. I constantly want to fight, but since I can't fight the Olive Skinned Man, I fight whoever is in front of me. I want to cry so hard until my eyes tear with blood. I have so much sorrow. I don't know how much longer I can keep this up. Please God help me before it's too late.

In my experience, we must take certain sequential steps for our minds to heal, and understanding guilt should be at the top of our list. *Guilt is like a putrid sludge that courses through our flesh.* It infects us with emotional distress and affects every important life decision we make until it resolves and washes away. But that's not the end of it. Our emotional distress will pass on to the ones we love, through our words and actions. I know firsthand how guilt causes us to become angry. Our anger accumulates over many years and we carry it around like a plague, transmitting it to everyone we meet. Is this any way to live? Isn't it time for us to relieve our guilt and anger and become truly healed?

You may be a friend or a relative of someone who suffered from violence or abuse. You may even feel indirectly responsible for not knowing that it was going to happen, or not doing enough to somehow prevent it. This is how I felt when the Olive Skinned Man violated us. As a consequence, we feel guilty. We feel we own the responsibility for the bad situations that happen to people we care about.

You may be the person who was attacked or abused and feel that in some way you provoked the onslaught which resulted in your own trauma. Like me, you've replayed the events in your mind hundreds of times, dissecting every second and trying to reconcile your own mistakes. What if I was more observant? What if I fought harder? Inevitably however, we conclude that we did something, or failed to do something which resulted in our trauma. This is especially true when those responsible for inflicting our pain have never seen justice. Of course, justice can mean different things to different people.

For two decades, I clutched to the unrealistic belief that I was somehow responsible for the outcome of that cold

November morning. As a manager, I believed I was accountable for everything and everyone in my charge. It enraged me to believe that one person could so easily destroy this reality in only a few minutes. For me, the emotional impact was even more intense because they weren't only my co-workers; they were my friends.

I constantly interrogated myself, revealing every possible error I made that day. I should've been listening to the angels warning me of the danger before I even entered the bank that morning. Maybe I shouldn't have reacted as I did when the Olive Skinned Man revealed his fake Uzi. Perhaps I should've talked to him and calmed him down, or rather jumped over my desk and attacked him to protect my friends. You see how these rationalizations create a false reality in which we're to blame.

Fortunately, the physical injuries my co-workers sustained were not life threatening and they left the hospital within several days. Of course, they still suffered the lasting effects of Trauma Induced Stress. When they were feeling well enough, they visited me in the hospital. I remember that day so clearly. When they walked into my room and I saw them for the first time after the shooting, I remember crying. I felt so remorseful that I couldn't protect them from the onslaught of Olive Skinned Man.

I know that many of you survivors reel from guilt, as I once did. The guilt we feel is intense and it stays with us for many years until it's finally resolved. Also, feelings of guilt don't dissipate or diminish simply through the passage of time. I've personally experienced two separate varieties of guilt which I call **Traumatic Guilt** and **Consequential Guilt**.

Traumatic Guilt is a feeling of culpability which derives out of our distorted belief that we acted, or neglected to act, in such a way as to cause our own trauma. With Traumatic Guilt, we strongly believe we caused the horrible events which led to our trauma.

I believe however that *Consequential Guilt* is even more powerful than Traumatic Guilt, especially when we have an emotional connection with the other individuals who've been physically or emotionally brutalized. It results when others suffer physical or emotional injuries consequential to the principal traumatic event. I've endured both Traumatic Guilt and Consequential Guilt for many years, until I discovered the only way to satisfy its need. I didn't find the cure in any doctor's office or book, but rather through my personal revelation. I believe that you deserve to experience your own revelation. The only question is, do you?

We are Survivors

I believe it is human nature to place blame, especially when those who caused our painful memories aren't caught to account for their actions. When I tell the story of that fateful day to someone for the first time, they sometimes ask me what I did to make the Olive Skinned Man shoot us. My outrage on this matter never fades. How can they believe that a man who's desperate enough to carry out armed federal bank robbery and the coldblooded shooting of three innocent people, is not responsible for the crime? How can they rather choose to blame me? How can people think that we got what we deserved because we must've done something to aggravate our attackers? Believe me, despite what people will say, you're not at fault. We weren't in control, we were unwilling participants.

The **First Step** each of us must take to begin healing is to recognize that we are survivors, not victims. *Victims have succumbed to defeat, and their spirit has been conquered and crushed. We survivors are fearless gladiators, and our spirit can never be broken. We survivors face life's challenges with strength and courage, and defeat is never an option. We are insulated by the Grace of God, for we are His faithful.* God feeds us and fills us up with his glory. He stands by our side and He never leaves us alone. Even in death, He sent Mother Mary to greet me and fill me with His Light. We are survivors because we have unshakable faith.

Terrible tragedies perpetrate themselves all around us, and by the grace of God, we are alive. We are not guilty of anything, we are survivors. I realize now that even though I took my responsibilities as a manager seriously, I could not have changed the outcome of that brutal November morning.

So please allow me to save you from years of similar anguish.

We are not responsible for our tragic circumstances. We acted the best way we knew how, given our level of experience and training. The Olive Skinned Man is the only person who is guilty of the actions he took that day, not me. You are also not to blame. You did your absolute best with the circumstances that were presented to you.

As survivors, we relinquish our feelings of guilt and free ourselves from this self inflicted pain. Unfortunately guilt does not resolve itself because we will it, and it does not go away over time. Resolving our feelings of guilt requires something dramatic and unexpected, but yet rather simple. Forgiving ourselves is the **Second Step** of healing and it can only be achieved through God and through an understanding that we are not to blame. So go ahead and forgive yourself for whatever you believe you did or didn't do to cause your trauma.

It was not long ago that I forgave myself for the mistakes I believed I made. I prayed to Our Lady of Mercy for wisdom, and She helped me to understand that I could free myself. I will always remember the cathartic uplifting I felt, when for the first time in more than twenty years, my feelings of guilt were swept away. I know that you survivors deserve the same, and I offer you these words so you may share my experience and purge yourself of guilt.

Closure & the Need for Vengeance

There is much to say about possibly the most elusive stage of Trauma Induced Stress, closure. It is the lack of closure that prevents us from moving forward with our lives in a substantially positive manner. I always believed that unless I could finish the chapter in my life, by finding the Olive Skinned Man and bringing him to justice, that I could not let go of my feelings of anger. So for many years I felt justified in feeling that I would one day come face to face with him. Any of us who has suffered from the tangible psychological effects of violent trauma call it the need for closure.

This requirement for so-called closure is merely a tidy expression we use for something much more visceral. It is in fact our excuse to hold on to the idea that we will one day get even. Justice however, is rarely achieved that satisfies our need for something more. Closure is our insatiable desire for vengeance. We feel warranted in the belief that we can and we will inflict the same variety of viciousness onto those responsible for our own pain. Yet despite our best efforts, we rarely achieve this kind of so-called closure. The complication arises out of the fact that we continue to harbor our insatiable desire for retribution. So in a poor attempt to satisfy our need for revenge, we inflict our insidious anger on those closest to us. How do you think these experiences will affect our children, especially when they have children of their own? Thankfully, there's a solution that replaces our insatiable desire for retribution with an overwhelming sense of tranquility.

I believe God created our everlasting souls, and that they belong to Him. I believe my soul was touched by evil. When the Olive Skinned Man exploded with his zealous rage on that cold November morning, he let loose the evil trapped within him. He transmitted his evil onto my soul and corrupted it. I believe our souls can become sickened and damaged by the evil around us, just as our bodies can become ill from the microscopic pathogens which manifest themselves as disease.

If you are like me and your soul is damaged, there is only one course of action to heal it and make it whole again. I have learned that God alone can cure our souls, driving out the evil that touched us. I believe that if we declare our acceptance of God into our body, our mind, and our soul and ask for His divine guidance, that He will surely heal us. I ask that you believe this and offer myself as the living proof of His healing power. Pray for God's intervention as I have and I promise that only good things will come of it.

Each of us survivors of trauma received a very special gift from God, which I call **Survivor's Perspective**. Our Survivor's Perspective is a powerful gift which we can embrace and use for the benefit of others, or we can choose to ignore it. But there is a catch. To use our special perspective, we must relinquish our feelings of anger and revenge. *Each of our personal harbingers of doom is in reality the Ark which has brought us to this unique place and given us our unique Survivor's Perspective.* Yet, how can we ever hope to appreciate our Survivor's Perspective when our perception is clouded by feelings anger and hopes of retribution?

*The road to Understanding must be walked with bare feet
And the path is paved with shards of glass.*

Jesus Prayer:
"Jesus Christ, the only Son of God, have mercy on me, a sinner."

No matter how strong our faith, we are all sinners. I am a sinner and you are a sinner. For many years after I was shot, I had trouble reconciling the passage in the Lord's Prayer that asks us to *"... forgive us our trespasses as we forgive those who trespass against us ..."* I repeatedly spoke to God through this prayer and struggled with what it was asking. I truly wanted God to forgive me of my sins, but how could He when I could not forgive the man who shot me. Enveloped with anguish and surrounded by pain, my mind struggled still.

My strong emotions of revenge and hate controlled me. I said to myself, "Who could blame me?" The Olive Skinned Man took my spleen, a kidney, some of my pancreas, and part of my lung and touched me with his evil. He left me for dead, lying on a concrete floor in a pool of spilled crimson blood. Even after 20 years, I am tortured each night by dreams of death, gore, and blood. I thought, "He is responsible for all of my problems and he deserves to die, right?" But why should any of this prevent me from forgiving the Olive Skinned Man?

The Lord's Prayer is simple, if I honestly forgive him, and ask God's forgiveness for my sins then God will forgive me. I know it doesn't feel simple when you are in pain. These may seem like a bunch of meaningless words that can't possibly ease the pain and anger that we've stewed into a brew of despair. But they are not just words, because I have learned that nothing is as powerful as God's Forgiveness.

My personal journey to forgive the Olive Skinned Man has been arduous. I have spent many years tormenting myself by searching for his face in every crowd and contemplating what I would do when I finally found him. It is what many years of feeling anger and vengeance will do to those of us who have been traumatized. Because of my previously un-reconciled hatred for the Olive Skinned Man, I also experienced vivid waking flashbacks of him firing his gun and killing me. These waking flashbacks occurred wherever I was, including my office or at home during family dinner. Flashbacks of the Olive Skinned Man are as real as any other person in the room and just as emotionally dramatic as the day it happened.

Please understand that a waking flashback is not an image in my mind. I can see my attacker in the room and he is as tangible as you. Every detail, from the bead of sweat running off the side of his face to the sound of the gunshot and the smell of burnt gunpowder, is as real as I am. My reaction is also just as real. It feels like experiencing the shooting again. I ask you, is holding on to our traumatic anger and vengeance worth the price of living like this? I believe it is time, with God's help, to forgive those responsible for our trauma. What do you think?

When my life became paralyzed with this new episode of Trauma Induced Stress, I became unable to function. It began with severe anxiety attacks, flashbacks of a gunman shooting at me, and nightmares of my murder in a hundred different ways. I call these deathmares. Soon after, I could no longer perform my job as a Vice President and Cash Management Sales Officer for The Bank of New York®.

As my symptoms worsened, I had no choice but to go on disability once again. My arms and legs started to tremor. I couldn't think anymore, and my mind became clouded and fuzzy. My muscles began to seize up and contract all at once causing great pain. Even the slightest sounds scared me to the point of collapse. The only place I felt even a little safe was my bedroom. I felt like my brain and body just stopped working altogether. It was so bad that I couldn't even interact with my own children.

By this time, my doctor prescribed an anti-anxiety medication called Xanax. For the next several months, I only became worse. Every sound I heard magnified 100 times louder inside my head. I lost the ability to phase out other voices in a room and to focus on the sound of only one person. I couldn't be in malls, restaurants, or parties. I was in pain, and confused. Doctors failed to help me as they increased the dosage of Xanax up to 12mg a day. When I wasn't angry and shouting I was depressed and crying.

With Maria's help, I sought aid from many skilled doctors including psychiatrists, psychologists and neurologists. I tried acupuncture, massage therapy, hyperbaric oxygen therapy and a variety of other holistic treatments, but with no avail. I even spent several days at the Lahey Clinic, but found no answers. These very real physical and emotional manifestations continued to spiral the lives of our whole family into oblivion.

My angel Maria stayed with me for every minute, but I know that it nearly destroyed her and our marriage with it. I could not understand why God saved me so many years before, only to allow me to suffer yet again. Perhaps I had more to learn, and perhaps pain is a good teacher. You have to realize that at the time, I had not yet forgiven the Olive Skinned Man for his actions. Also, I continued to bear the guilt which resulted from the shooting of my coworkers. Clearly, I had a lot to learn, and a lot to understand.

We didn't know what else to do. Finally, in December 2006, Maria and I called The Bank of New York® and begged them to help us. We explained how I continued to suffer from the apparent symptoms of Trauma Induced Stress caused from the shooting many years before. The Bank responded superlatively with assistance from one of their doctors. He told me that I first needed to get off this deadly drug called Xanax. He pointed out the only safe way to do it was under the constant care of medical professionals. Maria and I both agreed and so I took a trip to the Marworth Treatment Center in Waverly, PA, where I spent several weeks. I'd learn from these doctors that Xanax, a class of drugs called benzo-diazepines, is highly addictive and mind altering.

While coming off Xanax was challenging enough, the most difficult aspect I faced was being away from my family. At the time, Adam, Jessica, and Stephen were 9, 7, and 4 years old respectively. I called my family from a pay phone whenever I could. My most painful memory during this time was a partic-ular phone conversation with my four year old son, Stephen. I was reassuring him that I loved him, and then he asked me a question which felt like it wrenched my heart right out of my chest. He asked, "Daddy, are you dead?" For a moment, I gasped for breath and fell to my knees. I told him that I was very much alive and that I would see him soon. I knew he was too young to understand, yet tears were pouring down my face. All he knew was that his daddy wasn't there to hug him and kiss him good night. My life was in turmoil and my little boy thought I was dead. I thought once again, "Why would Our Lady save me and send me back from Heaven, if only to live a hell here on earth?"

It's curious though, how the path from reliving my trau-ma took me to this place. Here I was, surrounded by people from all walks of life with addictions to alcohol and drugs. These were essentially good people, just like you and I, who became trapped by a chemical addition. On one particular day I found myself talking to a young man named Seth about his addiction to drugs. Seth told me about the crimes he com-mitted and the people he hurt to get money for his addiction.

As our conversation continued he became emotionally enraged, and I saw for only the second time in my life, the same expression of rage so intense that he could kill some-one! It was the very same unmistakable expression of the Ol-ive Skinned Man who shot me and left me for dead those many years ago. I became terrified and made an excuse to walk away and calm down.

I suppose I owe Seth a debt of gratitude for helping me finally understand the singular and most pronounced question of all, why did he shoot us? I began to understand. I believe the Olive Skinned Man also had a drug or alcohol addiction. I now also realize that he would have done anything to get money to support his addiction. But what's more was my realization that I could become just like Seth or the Olive Skinned Man, unless a significant change occurred. I began to understand that these events were taking place in response to my prayers for wisdom, and remembered Our Lady's promise that She'd always be with me to guide me.

A few days later, a recovered drug addict named Doug came to speak to us about how he ruined his life before he got clean and sober. He began trying to make an emotional connection with the audience by describing all the horrible acts he committed to get money to support his addition. Doug told us that his addiction altered his mind and his thoughts to the point where nothing else was important, including his wife Beth, his two children and his job. He said the only thing that was important was getting high and staying high. He told us that he started by borrowing money from his friends and family members, but when they realized the money was for drugs, they quickly cut him off. Doug said he didn't let that stop him from getting money, and he soon stepped up to robbing jewelry and electronics from the homes of the same friends and family members. He said it was easy money because he already knew what they owned and where they kept it. He just waited until they were asleep or out of the house to pull the job.

I could already see some of the audience members beginning to relate with Doug's story, and he was about to kick it into high gear. Then he said, when there was nothing left to steal from his family and friends, he didn't think twice about buying an illegal gun to commit armed robberies of convenience stores and deli's. He even admitted to shooting a clerk in the arm, but said he never paid for the act. Doug said he soon learned this approach wasn't as easy as he expected since some of the store owners had guns of their own and were willing to shoot back. He was rallying up to his big finish, and so he shouted loudly to incite the audience and questioned; "How many of you've thought about getting a gun and robbing a bank to get money for your addiction?" More than a few people raised their hands and cheered him in response to his question. I bet Doug felt like a rock star at that moment, but I just felt horrified and a little disgusted.

For me, there were no more questions about the motives of the Olive Skinned Man. I believe God gave me this experience to relive my anguish. I believe He sent me on a journey to this place so I might understand the feelings and motives behind the man who changed my life forever. This is why I thank God each day for the goodness and the sadness. These experiences truly make us who we are. Please do not be angry with God. Rather, embrace every moment with clarity because I believe there is a purpose for it all.

God offered me enlightenment by showing me how the pieces fit together. I still had to complete the puzzle. I finally realized that to use my God-given Survivor's Perspective, I needed to divest myself of my overwhelming feelings of anger and hatred caused by my unsatisfied need for revenge. I knew I had to forgive the Olive Skinned Man of his sins against me. I knew that by absolving him, my own pain would wash away.

The key that will open the gateway to unburden our anger can only be forged through understanding. So the **Third Step** in our healing is to conscientiously understand the pain of those who have hurt us. I know this idea feels dramatically contrary to our nature and difficult to appreciate, but stay with me. Our experiences give us perspective, but our anger and feelings of revenge only distort our minds. In turn, we pass our anger to others, even the ones we love and vow to protect. Over time, our anger will become pervasive and incendiary. At these heights, it will consume everything in its path. I know firsthand how our anger can transform us into a version of the person who first touched our lives with evil!

As there is goodness, so is there evil. If we can understand their pain, then perhaps we can make sense of what drove them to act heinously. If we can understand why, then perhaps we can forgive them for their sins. This is a chief principal. With God as our witness, we must endeavor to forgive those we blame for causing our living nightmare. This is the **Fourth Step** in our healing.

Please consider my perspective. I believe the person who hurt me as well as those who have hurt you deserve our forgiveness. I know how angry you must feel right now, that I would even suggest they warrant our forgiveness. But I believe that the individuals who have inflicted pain on us are survivors of the same variety of pain. The difference between us is, they did not choose to embrace their gift of perspective and they could never find forgiveness for those who hurt them.

I have come to a point in my own life where I have not only forgiven the Olive Skinned Man who shot me, but even more than that. I am grateful to him for emancipating me from a life of shallow thought and inequity. We are all the same, and we all deserve God's forgiveness. I never saw the Olive Skinned Man again after that cold morning in November of 1990 and I don't know if he's alive or dead. So how could I forgive him and more importantly, how can you forgive those who are responsible for your own painful anger?

First let me say that trying to forget about these events over time will never relieve your pain. Rather, we must embrace our pain like a warm blanket. We must accept it, because let's face it; the memory is not going away. Even after twenty years, my rage for revenge was stronger than ever. It wasn't until I reconciled my anger with forgiveness that I could find peace in my heart. Since then, a new world of perspective has opened for me. It was like a secret door unlocked and revealed a world of treasures for me. The secret door was always right in front of me, but I ignored it. Your secret door is right in front of you, and when you are prepared to honestly forgive the sins of others, all you have to do is walk through it and be healed.

It is only when this happens, that you will be released from your own burdens of hatred and revenge. Remember, our feelings of anger do not make us stronger nor do they insulate us against additional negative feelings. Only by allowing God into our lives will we gain the understanding we require to shed our feelings of anger and revenge that we have harbored for so many years. Like me, you may have never known the identity of the person responsible for your anguish, and it may seem difficult to understand their motives. Yet, it matters little. It is imperative to forgive them and then thank them for giving you a Survivor's Perspective on a new life, a life where you are powerful and kind. Powerful to impact the lives of others you meet with your Survivor's Perspective.

Your understanding of another's life and motivation is something that may take months or even years to achieve. Yet I urge you to take the time to gain wisdom and personal revelation about the most painful events in your lives. You can choose to hold your anger inside and despise others for hurting and ruining your life. After all, that's your right, isn't it? Hell, that's exactly what I did for nearly twenty years. Yet I'll tell you that these ill feelings you harbor will have exacting negative consequences on nearly every decision you make in your life.

You take your anger and use it against other's who do not deserve it. Then, they will carry it and pass it along to someone else, and so on. Some of the affected may be your own children. They say that these tendencies are passed down through genetics, but isn't it more likely that these behaviors are passed down through reinforcement. I know that at first you will deny what I say is true, but in time you too will understand that *Forgiveness is truly the greatest expression of revenge.*

I know that what I am asking sounds like a leap of faith and it is. But couldn't we all use a little more faith; all you have to do is believe. If you believe in God, He will believe in you. Then, anything at all is possible, even what we call miracles. Trust me when I tell you that my faith in God has given me the strength, the will, the power and the opportunity to create the greatest life anyone could hope for. I thank God for allowing me to experience death, pain, anguish, and forgiveness. Because I now have a perspective that most people could never imagine. How could I possibly appreciate the joy of living that I can experience with each new day, without knowing dread, horror, and anguish?

My Symbol of Our Lady of Mercy

Three years after the shooting, I had the bullet that caused most of my internal injuries removed from the muscle in my back. Soon after, I brought it to I. Friedman & Son Jewelers, located at 10 West 47th Street, and asked my friend Rob to mount it, so I could wear it on a chain. Today I wear the bullet around my neck, right next to my crucifix. At first, my family did not understand why I would wear a symbol of what they believed was pain and destruction. They did not see it the way that I did. To me, the bullet is a symbol of hope and salvation. I believe it is surely the bullet that Our Lady of Mercy sent to me that saved my life. The bullet is my symbol of Mother Mary, and I wear it proudly on my chain next to my symbol of Her son, Jesus Christ.

On one particular day, a few years later, I was sitting in a doctor's office and picked up a magazine to pass the time. I found myself reading the story about the attempted assassination of His Holiness, Pope John Paul II in 1981, and learned a few things I never knew. The shooting occurred on May 13th, which is the Feast of Our Lady of Fatima. The Pope believed that Our Lady of Fatima was responsible for saving his life. The Pope said "It was a mother's hand that guided the bullet's path." As a result, John Paul II traveled to Fatima, Portugal and presented the bullet to the Bishop of Leira-Fatima who enshrined it into the crown of the statue of Our Lady of Fatima. This single act transformed a symbol of death into a symbol of faithful maternal protection. This story only reinforced my belief that Our Lady of Mercy guided the bullet that saved my own life.

Like me, you have a unique perspective on every event that happens in your life and in the lives of those around you. You have earned this perspective. Do not squander it by getting caught in the mire and pessimism of those around you. Use your gift. Yes, your gift. I believe that your tragedy, like mine, is a precious gift from God. Our priceless gift gives us incredible perspective on what is truly important in our *New Lives*. Use your special gift to create the world around you that you deserve. Using your God-given Survivor's Perspective to create a New Life is the **Fifth Step** in our healing.

It took me twenty years to understand, but believe me. The act of forgiving your nemesis as I have forgiven the Olive Skinned Man will heal you and offer you a sense of peace and strength that you have never felt before. If you think this idea seems contrary to our normal reaction to harbor hatred all of our lives for those who imposed us with anguish, then you are correct. We must make a paradigm shift in the way we understand healing. For, if we cannot shed these hateful feelings of anger and desires of revenge, we simply will never heal. Also, since we are only human and sin on occasion, how can we receive God's forgiveness unless we forgive those who have sinned against us? When you have practiced this tool successfully, you will be able to unwrap and fully employ your special gift of Survivor's Perspective.

My fellow survivors, we share a great deal in common. We've seen the grim visage of evil himself and live today in spite of it. The plans we once had for the future have been indelibly altered by this experience. But in its place, we are offered a new future and a heavenly endowment. See it, grasp it, and take great advantage of your Survivor's Perspective. We understand that people and our relationships with them are important. We understand that love is stronger than hate, and we rely on these principles to live our lives.

My Survivor's Perspective

The following story, serves as my constant reminder of what happens when people fail to value human life before monetary wealth. On one particular Friday afternoon in March of 2012, I had a business meeting with a man named Mark. He began to tell me about a client he just saw, whose son-in-law committed suicide during the previous Thanksgiving holiday, leaving his wife and two young children. Mark told me the young man apparently hung himself at his father-in-law's house, inside the garage.

I could not help think to myself how emotionally distraught this man must have been. How could he feel as though he had nothing more to live for, and with no option or assistance from family, other than to kill himself? Mark went on to describe how the son-in-law was so callous to leave his wife and children, and on Thanksgiving as well. I also learned that the son-in-law was not doing well financially. He asked his father-in-law to borrow $400,000 on his primary residence, so he could buy distressed properties and flip them at a profit.

Mark explained how his client's son-in-law was so selfish and heartless, that he had the arrogance to leave his wife without a husband, his children without a father, and his father-in-law with a pile of debt. To top it all off, this inconsiderate dead man forever ruined his entire family's Thanksgiving holiday and acted so cold-heartedly to kill himself in his father-in-law's house and not his own.

What is the undeniable truth that is clearly missing from this story, and how is it that these people are oblivious to it? A man is dead! His life on this earth is forever over and no one seems to care. So, will the real selfish, heartless, arrogant and cold-blooded people please stand up? Are we so raveled up in our own lives, with our homes, cars, Hi-Definition TV's and Smartphone's that we have absolutely gone insane?

When was it, exactly, in the timeline of human existence, that we as a race of humans put objects before other people? It infuriates me, as it should you. This young man who killed himself was in trouble emotionally and needed the support of his family and friends. I do not mean with money but with understanding, compassion, and direction. Someone close to him must have known how emotionally depressed and suicidal he was. Why didn't someone hold him by the hand and get him help? If he was abusing alcohol or other drugs, why didn't someone pick him up and bring him to rehabilitation? And most of all, why didn't someone pick him up and bring him to God?

Regardless of your own particular religion, God is God. You may call Him by another name, but I believe we are praying to the same God. And it is only through Him that we will be healed. Trust me on this, I am His living proof. Of course we should love God first, and then please always place people on the top of your list of priorities, or this might happen to someone you care about.

I am just an ordinary man who has had some extraordinary experiences. I am no more special than you are. I have learned greatly from my experiences, and believe that every one of us has a greater purpose in our lives. Rather than taking all we can get our hands on, we ought to give back to those who need it more than we do. Whether you offer love, friendship, a helping hand, or simply a hug, please consider other people even before you consider yourself, especially strangers. I promise you will become a better and happier person because of it. All you have to do is listen to His signs and then act on them. ***Remember that knowledge alone is not power. Only knowledge plus action is power.*** So, do something to make the world around you a better place, and if you have the opportunity, save someone's life.

It is this perspective that constantly reminds me what is important in my life, other people. We should all remember that God wants us to be better to each other. I believe we should put people much higher on our list of what is important. Once we realize that people are more important than riches and we decide to do something about it, then the world will become a better place. This is my Survivor's Perspective.

Chapter Six
SEIZING OPPORTUNITY RE-SHAPED

L ike many of you, I believed opportunity was something
we should always take advantage of, especially when it
benefited us. So all our lives, we have taken the opportunity
to succeed in school, sports, business, and love. Seizing opportunities helped us get that big promotion, which trans-
lated into more money in our pockets. Seizing opportunities
helped us to marry the person of our dreams, and to raise the
children we always wanted. Seizing opportunity has surely
brought us great benefits. But through the many years of trial
and tribulation, God's given me a new understanding of how
opportunity should be used, and for whom.

We are constantly offered opportunities which we either
do not see or simply ignore. These are the opportunities to
help not ourselves, but others. Some of them are people we
know, and some are complete strangers. By the way, I believe
the word "stranger", in current day terms, has gotten a bad
rap. We learned growing up that a stranger is a person who

might harm us, and that we should avoid them at all costs. Remember what our parents and teachers taught at an early age about "stranger danger" and why we should always run away from them.

While it is true that predators and scam artists exist, it is equally true that there are many decent people like you and me, who simply need a little help. But what's the point? Why bother getting involved in the lives of strangers who don't mean anything to us? If we are not getting money, sex, or food in return, then what's in it for us? At a glance, the answer appears to be absolutely nothing. However I believe we must seize the opportunity to help others we meet because people, not money, are the most important resource on this planet, and our collective futures depend on it. Remember, people are not the disease, indifference is the disease.

I believe the human race is at war, and our eternal souls are the spoils of that war. We are all fighting with an enemy so elusive, that his greatest trick is making us believe he doesn't even exist. Many of us already firmly believe in a benevolent God who helps us to become better people. Then you must understand that as genuine and powerful as God is, there exists his antithesis. Satan is God's pernicious and malevolent counterpart.

Satan is a powerful adversary who would have us fighting each other, and he would be perfectly content with our apathetic indifference of human kind. Satan's most powerful weapons include hatred, anger, greed, and the desire for us to worship material objects. For how can we emulate the love taught to us by Jesus Christ, if we are too busy hating each other. And how can we devote ourselves to God if we're too busy worshiping the so called almighty dollar. Money comes and money goes, but God is with us forever. Satan has distracted us from what's supremely important, and it's time we realized that we should care for each other more than we care for riches, because people are the true wealth of this world.

Like many of you, God offered me opportunities to help others which I ignored. I failed to act because I was indifferent or afraid that harm might come to me. I'm not proud of these failures, but with the help of the Lord, they've taught me to become a more caring person. The steep road I've walked and sometimes fallen down on, has shown me that people are willing to rise to the occasion and inconvenience themselves for the benefit of others. And sometimes, I was the one who needed helping. These true stories have shaped my new life and the man that I have become.

A Stranger's Valiant Sacrifice

On one particular night during my 11 weeks in the hospital, a stranger's self-sacrifice saved my life. My doctors had to perform a surgical procedure called a thoracotomy to remove an infection in my chest. The doctors described the operation to my family as very bloody and dangerous. After hearing this, my parents asked for a second surgical opinion but no other doctors in the hospital would impede the opinion of my primary surgeon, for fear of consequences. With no other option my parents thought of the only surgeon outside of Winthrop Hospital that they knew.

In September of 1990, my father underwent open heart bypass surgery. The surgeon who performed the operation was the Chief of Cardiothoracic Surgery at North Shore University Hospital in Manhasset. My father's triple bypass surgery was a complete success and the brilliant surgeon who performed the operation was Dr. Anthony Tortolani. Aside from this one-time doctor/patient relationship, my father and Dr. Tortolani were apparent strangers. So on this particular chilly winter evening, my parents desperately reached out to the North Shore University Hospital in hopes of contacting Dr. Tortolani to obtain his help.

Of course, I had no idea this was all going on until an unexpected visitor entered my hospital room. It was late and my room was dimly lit. As he entered through the doorway, the bright lights from the hallway behind illuminated his silhouette like some sort of angel of mercy. I remember looking at the clock, it was just after midnight. I was already wide awake, but I still didn't understand why a man dressed in a black tuxedo was visiting me in the middle of the night.

When he introduced himself, I remembered the name of

the man who operated on my father only a few months before. He told me that my parents asked him to take a look at me before my surgery as a precaution. I thanked him for seeing me so late, but asked why he was dressed in a tuxedo. Dr. Tortolani told me that he left his own birthday party to see me, and he'd be returning to it as soon as he visually examined me. I wished him a very happy birthday, and as he left my room I saw him talking to my parents in the hallway. I later learned he told them that he wouldn't expect me to survive the scheduled operation, and that I should be physically stronger before attempting it. As a result, my parents postponed the operation until I was stronger.

So on that particular night, Dr. Anthony Tortolani became one of my personal heroes. You see, he had the opportunity to remain at his birthday party, eating good food and enjoying the company of his family and friends. Yet, he chose a different path. He chose the opportunity to leave these comforts at his personal inconvenience and travel to a hospital room in the dead of night to save the life of a complete stranger. Dr. Tortolani never asked for a penny of compensation in return for his valiant sacrifice. With such goodness, how can anyone not believe in God? His selfless actions that night had a tremendous impact in shaping the man I am today. Ever since, I've tried to uphold his flawless example, even when it was inconvenient for me.

The Two Angels

On one particular day in August of 1991, my family and I were vacationing in Bermuda. My parents took Pete and me on a cruise to help us dampen the worst days of our lives. The cruise ship provided the perfect environment for my continued recuperation. The day after we arrived in Hamilton, we took a shuttle bus to my favorite beach on the planet, Horseshoe Bay Beach. As if its fine white sandy beach with tall rock outcroppings along the shore weren't enough to ensure a picturesque backdrop to a perfect setting, the ebb and flow of its turquoise nectar gently caressed the shore like a mother strokes her child. If heaven exists on earth, I always thought this must be it.

Smack in the middle of the bay lay a huge rock jutting twenty five feet, straight out of the water. We'd been here many times over the years and we always swam out to the rock, climbed up and jumped off. So on this particular day, Pete, Dad and I all started the swim to the rock. My enthusiasm however, got the best of me. As we reached the halfway point, my body became so exhausted that I couldn't take even a single stroke more. With my muscles still weakened from the 11 weeks of languish, I tried desperately to catch my breath long enough before my body sank below the surface for the first time.

I struggled back atop the water and called to my brother Pete for help. Pete was a body builder and had remarkable endurance, but before he could reach me, I slipped beneath the surface yet again. As I sank further, I fought as hard as I could to lift my arms above my head. I'll never forget feeling my brother's hand as he reached down and pulled me out from a most certain watery grave. With my limp body in tow, we three began back to shore. Pete and I became separated from our

Dad, and we didn't realize until we reached the beach that he also began to drown.

He told us later that no one was near him to hear his cries for help. He said he thought it was all over for him, but suddenly a man came out of nowhere, rescued him from drowning and helped him to shore. He remembers lying on his back too weak to stand and spitting up water. When he opened his eyes to see the man who saved him, he vanished as quickly as he first appeared. It was early in the morning and we were the only ones on the beach. Yet, we couldn't find the man anywhere. If you just seized the opportunity to save someone from drowning, then swam them to shore and carried them on the beach, wouldn't you stay for even a minute? Wouldn't you make sure they didn't need CPR, or at least wait until a family member appeared? You would, wouldn't you? I believe an Angel sent from Heaven saved my Dad that day.

Angels do exist, and I believe they walk among us. God does love us and I believe He is leading us, not only by the example set by His son Jesus, but also by the example set by his Angels. I will always remember the two angels that helped us that day, one whose name is a whisper in the wind and the other is my brother Pete. I'm not suggesting that Pete is an Angel from Heaven, but that his actions were angelic. We should all follow their example and help others in need, even at our own person risk. I believe random acts of selflessness fuel our souls with goodness and deal a hearty blow to Satan. For, if we don't act righteously, Satan will be one step closer to claiming our immortal souls. That day, goodness won the battle. The time to choose is right now. Which side will you fight for?

The Water's Edge

In the summer of '77 and on one particular sunny afternoon, I was fishing by a lake in the Florida Everglades. Every year our parents took us on vacation to Florida, and this year was no different, or so I thought. We traveled in our 'Yellow Submarine' motor home and we stopped in one of our usual campgrounds for the day. Mom was fixing lunch and Dad was hooking up the utilities. Tom and Pete suggested we do a little exploring and collect some fire wood for the evening blaze. Normally that sounded like a great idea but I remember getting this image in my head that I needed to be by the lake fishing.

So there I was fishing pole in hand, standing by a lake full of fish and... alligators. I knew enough to steer clear of the water's edge and keep a close eye on the gators floating just under the surface. They looked a little like floating wooden logs, but they were gators alright. I continued fishing for about an hour, but I didn't catch a single one. It was almost 2:00 and I knew that Mom wanted us all back for lunch by then. I sent my final cast way out and it landed in the water right next to one of the gators floating on the surface. As soon as it splashed down, the gator swam under the water to get away.

I reeled in the line, picked up my tackle box and started back. I was almost on the trail when I spotted a man on the other side of the lake. I took a closer look, expecting to see him holding a fishing rod or binoculars to check out the wildlife, but he wasn't. I knew right away that something bad was about to happen. You see, this middle aged tourist wore nothing but a bathing suit and a white bath towel draped over his bare shoulders. I dropped my gear and shouted at him to stop, but he was too far away to hear me and he just waved back.

I started to run around the lake as fast as I could. He looked at me and must've thought I was just a crazy kid waving my arms and shouting, so he ignored me as he dropped his towel and moved closer to the water's edge. Just then, he stepped up onto a small boulder by the shore and prepared to jump in the water. I needed to get there faster so I ran closer than I should have to the water's edge to make up ground. I could see those gators eyeing me, but this guy was about to become bait, so I kept going.

When I finally reached him, I took a deep breath and shouted, "Stop!" He stepped off the rock and asked me what was going on. I said "Before you go swimming in the lake, I want to show you something." I told him to keep his eye on the floating log about twenty feet from the water's edge. Then I reached down, picked up a stone, and threw it at the log. When it thrashed in the water and submerged, he looked at me and said, "What was that?" Then I pointed out all the hungry alligators catching the sun's rays.

He turned white as a ghost and said, "I'd be dead right now if it wasn't for you!" He thanked me over and over, but I just told him that I was late for lunch and had to go. I never got his name, and I never thought twice about what I had to do, I just did it. Thinking back, I believe God or his angelic messengers put that image of fishing at the lake in my mind, so I could be there at the right time. Will you be there at the right time when it's your turn?

In Harm's Way

It was a warm summer night in '94. It was late and I'd just gotten off the Number 2 Express Train from Manhattan and walked toward Penn Station to catch a train home. The subway tunnel looked nearly deserted. There were five young guys dressed in jeans and hooded sweatshirts walking twenty feet ahead of me. Just ahead of them was a young woman walking and dressed like she was also returning from work in Manhattan. It felt to me like they intended to harm the young woman, and when I got closer, I overheard them saying as much. I was now certain that they were going to attack her.

Outnumbered, I had the opportunity to back off and protect myself from injury, or the opportunity to place myself in harm's way and help a complete stranger. They knew I was right behind them, so one of them slowed down to intercept me. But fueled with the recollection of how others saved me at their personal expense, I didn't let one man slow me down. I dealt with the laggard and moved ever closer to the gang.

The young woman realized she was in trouble and began to run away. These guys were looking for easy prey, and my presence was enough to disburse them from continuing their attack on her. They stopped and turned to me, and as I walked straight through the bunch, they remarked, "Okay hero, you won this one." And it was over. I got on the train to go home, but I never saw the young woman again. If you ask me if God exists, I'll tell you He's as real as Satan. So if we don't fight against the evil which lurks in the hearts of men, then Satan might win the war for our immortal souls. I believe we can't afford to lose. What do you believe?

Shattering the Barriers

On one particular day, I had the opportunity to make a big difference. My choice to accept and seize this opportunity was one that would eventually save the lives of many people working or doing business in retail bank branches. Working in banks for more than twenty years taught me volumes about bank security. Even before the robbery that ended in my shooting, I'd come to a definitive realization about the use of bullet resistant acrylic barriers, sometimes called bandit barriers. Banks place these barriers between the tellers' area and the bank floor to protect their assets. I've worked in every capacity of retail banking including teller, so I understand what it feels like on both sides of the bandit barrier.

As a young teller working for The Dime Savings Bank of New York, I felt safer working behind a thick acrylic wall, but I'd later come to realize this was a false sense of security. In fact, my experience demonstrated that bandit barriers only elevate the brutal nature of bank robbers. The barriers encourage them to take extreme measures to accomplish their goal. Keep in mind that I'm not referring to whether these barriers reduce the incidence of bank robberies, but rather that these barriers strongly elicit an escalated level of violence.

Because of this, I believe bank employees and customers are at increased risk. In my estimation, if bank robbers want the cash behind the glass badly enough, then they'll attempt to get it by any means necessary. Never the less, this is only one man's educated opinion and I never expected one man could make a difference regarding an issue with such far reaching scope, until one day...

In August of 2009, I received a priority mail letter from a man named Lawrence Sherman, PhD, who's a Wolfson

Professor of Criminology at Cambridge University in England. The letter said he needed my help to stop a proposed local law, No. 960-A that would mandate implementing bandit barriers in banks throughout New York City.

His credentials asserted him to have over forty years of experience in research, police executive education, and public policy analysis. He's also worked as a civilian research analyst in the New York City Police Department, and has collaborated with police and criminal justice agencies around the world. According to Professor Sherman's letter, research suggests that bullet resistant enclosures around tellers' areas may increase the risks of injury to bank employees working outside the enclosed area, as well as to customers.

Professor Sherman said that he and other prominent authorities already gave testimony to the New York City Council against proposed law 960-A, but with no avail. He said the Council was still in favor of passing the new law, and was sure my testimony would weigh enough to change the balance, and prevent the law from passing. His letter closed by apologizing for reminding me of the horrific events that nearly took my life, but asked if I would contact him by phone to discuss the matter.

The effects of Trauma Induced Stress were already controlling many facets of my life. So the idea of an interview to rehash the very details I wanted nothing more to do with was not at all appealing. Of course the toughest decisions are also the most life changing and perhaps getting involved would give me the strength I needed to move forward. Could one man's opinion really make a difference? I was about to find out. I called Professor Sherman and we agreed to meet as soon as he could travel to Long Island.

One afternoon we met for about an hour in a conference room near my home. I thanked him for allowing me to voice my opinion on such an important issue, in hopes of saving lives. In a recorded interview Professor Sherman asked me pointed questions regarding my more than twenty years of banking experience. I detailed my general work experience as well as that which related to my direct knowledge of bank robberies.

I began by recounting the events of the bank robbery and multiple shootings which took place in Garden City Park on November 29th 1990. I stated that this single unmasked robber knew we had a lot of cash and wasn't going to let a plastic wall stop him from getting it. All he needed was a gun and a helping of anger. I told Professor Sherman that I firmly believed the very presence of a bandit barrier actually elicits a higher level of violence toward anyone who isn't behind the barrier. However, once the bandit gets behind the barrier, the tellers aren't protected either.

I told him that in my experience, bandit barriers don't stop bank robbers from getting their loot. They're desperate and they'll devise any means to defeat the barrier; whatever the cost to them or to us. We make rules that we expect people to follow. But they have their own set of rules, and they don't care who they hurt or kill. Professor Sherman asked me if I thought the robbery would've happened differently if there'd been no resistant glass. I said, "Without the barrier, the robbery would've been much less violent."

There are dozens of procedures that banks can employ to reduce the incidence of theft and injury to its customers and employees without the use of bullet resistant walls. These barriers ultimately promote a high level of violence. So, in my opinion, if the new law passed, you could expect violent bank robberies to increase dramatically.

Professor Sherman also asked me to describe my experience working with the Seamen's Bank for Savings in New

York City. I indicated that I was the Sales Manager for three branches, including offices on Wall Street, Beaver Street and Pine Street. Each branch had full video surveillance and bandit barriers. Between 1988 and 1989 there was a bank robbery in one of those three branches every two weeks. While many of them were harmless note-passers, many still were vicious robbers armed with pistols and shotguns, and they were not averse to using them.

Once, in our Wall Street branch, a man robbed one of our tellers with a shoebox bomb. He placed the box on the counter, just outside the bandit barrier and threatened to explode the bomb remotely unless he received cash and could walk out of the bank safely. You see, the bandits expect to get the money, escape freely, and remain safe. They are not interested in the safety of anyone else. So despite video surveillance cameras and security guards, he successfully robbed the bank, strolled across Wall Street, and escaped into the subway. He would've blown us all up if he felt threatened. This incident is a powerful example of how a bullet resistant barrier, with the purpose of protecting and reducing theft, only incites criminals to greater heights of violence.

I also recounted the incidence of six extremely violent robberies which occurred at the Pine Street branch in a similar manner. This secluded area of Pine Street didn't see much auto or pedestrian traffic. The interior of the branch was small and was easy to control, especially by an organized group of armed criminals. There were two desks on the platform, for the Branch Manager and Customer Service Representative. Also, there were four teller stations enclosed behind a bullet resistant barrier. The Pine Street branch is located directly behind Wall Street branch and interestingly enough, the two branches were connected through a series of walkways.

In each incident, three men with pistols and shotguns took the manager by surprise and struck him repeatedly on the head and body with the butt of their shotgun. The thugs threatened to shoot him if anyone pulled the silent alarm. The bandits then forced the manager to open the door and gain entry to the tellers' unit. Once inside, they also pistol-whipped several tellers causing more serious head wounds. Soaked in their own blood and forced to empty all the cash drawers into a duffel bag, the bank staff remained helpless as the bandits escaped freely.

In each case, the bank employees suffered severe physical and traumatic injuries. One of the tellers named Elise was three months pregnant with her first child. After one of the robberies she was missing for over an hour. She saw the bandits coming in the front door and hid in a small supply closet. We finally found Elise curled up in a ball on the floor behind a stack of boxes. Terrorized, she couldn't move or even speak for hours. In each of these violent armed robberies, the main deterrent was the bullet resistant enclosure surrounding the bank tellers and the cash. I told Professor Sherman in my testimony that in my experienced opinion, it wouldn't have gone down that way if there wasn't a bandit barrier.

In the interview, Professor Sherman told me that my testimony was so powerful and significant, that it alone should prevent proposition 960-A from passing into law. He said that when The New York City Council reads it, they will fully understand the reality and the potential danger that bandit barriers pose. I finished the interview by saying although the memory of my shooting isn't easy to talk about; I felt that I must testify if it could save even one human life.

I heard from Professor Sherman one week later. He called to thank me and say that my testimony had single-handedly prevented Proposition 960-A from passing into law. Also, I never asked for compensation, nor did I receive any for my testimony. I did it to save lives.

In October of 2013, I sent Professor Sherman a letter. I thanked him for helping me realize that while the shooting has changed me, it's also made me more experienced and valuable than I was before. My opportunity to save others was a turning point in my recovery, and it showed me that my traumatic experience shouldn't be forgotten, but rather savored. I believe there is no such thing as coincidence. Just as God called me to help others, I believe He wants you to do the same. We each have a reason for being, and sometimes it is only through pain that we discover our true purpose in life. What do you think?

Chapter Seven
OUR FUTURE IS TODAY

Our only true future is today. The past is gone forever and tomorrow may never come, so pay attention to today and enjoy it.

We are no longer constrained to live life the way society dictates. We know we must live our lives in the moment that is today, because anything else is foolishness. So one day at a time, and with the grace of God, we do our best to help others in need. We share our Survivor's Perspective with others who are weighed down by a pile of negative thoughts and emotions, and try to enlighten them the way we have been. For me, living for today isn't just an expression; it's a way of life. I used to expend so much of my mental energy thinking about next month and next year, but it didn't occur to me to focus on where I was that moment. So, I wasted many precious years. Please understand, our past is over and our future has yet to be written, so our whole world exists right now in this very moment. I think we should spend our moments wisely and well. What do you think?

The events of my protracted hospitalization and subsequent recuperation forced me to transform the way in which

I perceived my future in life. Before November 29, 1990, I had my whole life planned out. I planned months and years ahead, but never looking where I was right now. Even more, when I wasn't living my life in the future, I was living it in the past, convinced that thinking about today was pointless. I was an A-Type personality with long-range goals, and the image of a target with a bull's-eye was firmly etched into my mind. I was a man with a plan.

Today, I am still a man with a plan, except my future is right in front of me. I suppose God did not have the same future for me as I did. I have learned to look at life in the moment. I know we talk about smelling the proverbial roses, and from time to time we may actually live for today, but we rarely practice it as a way of life. *Brutal experience has no room for a future in which we discount the present.* We must depart from our old ways of excluding actual living for the scarlet dreams which we may never realize.

But exactly how was it that I made such a paradigm shift and came to this realization? Sure, the tragic shooting and my visit to Heaven had a lot to do with it, but eventually I began to revert to my old ways of living in the future. What I needed was a constant. I needed something that would show me the reason slowing down and living life for today was better. So Our Lady of Mercy sent me on another journey, to meet the woman who would teach me a better way to live.

With each new day I endeavor to thank God and Our Lady of Mercy for saving me. With each rising sun I am given the courage to lift my head once more, sometimes still with much agony. Yet, the rewards bestowed have been even greater than all the pain and devastation combined.

On one particular day in October of '91 I heard the sweet reverberating tone of the woman who'd become my best friend, my wife, and surely my angel sent by God. I was back to work part-time in my newly created position as Sales Coach for the staff of The Bank's Long Island retail branches. On this particular day, I found myself at the branch in Port Washington where I coordinated my days schedule with the Branch Manager, Joyce Martin (now Joyce Martin Forrler).

Joy and I had a lot in common and we became quick friends working together over the previous weeks. It was the middle of the afternoon and I'd just completed a sales coaching session with Joy's staff. We were on the bank floor when she asked me if I'd like to meet her good friend Maria. I'd come to respect Joy's opinion, besides she only had wonderful things to say about Maria, so I agreed. I never expected her though, to pick up the phone and dial Maria on the spot. When Maria answered, Joy told her there was someone she wanted her to meet, and then surprised us both when she handed me the phone. That's classic Joy, living for today!

I didn't want to embarrass Maria or myself, so I asked to call her back later that night. I called Maria around 9 p.m. and we had a fantastic conversation, culminating in a plan for our first date that Friday night. After we hung up, I had a feeling this might turn out to be something special, and I'd learned to trust my intuition. Who knows, maybe God was telling me something. Perhaps Maria would be the woman of my dreams. Just in case she was, I'd keep my heart and soul open for any signs from above.

On Friday night, November 1st 1991, (11/1 The Beginning), I drove to Maria's home in New Hyde Park. I arrived early in anticipation of our date but parked around the corner until the scheduled time. I've always had a habit of being on time wherever I went. I learned early on that if you're not fifteen minutes early then you've already missed the opportunity, whatever it is. Since I was early I figured Maria might still be getting ready, so I waited. I must've checked my watch forty times in a futile effort to somehow, will time to move faster.

At 8 p.m. and with a bouquet of fresh flowers in hand, I walked up to her door and lightly knocked. When she opened it, I was captivated by the breathtaking beauty that stood before me. Her long undulating brown hair flowed over her shoulders and her dark eyes swelled with enchantment. I thought, "Don't be too anxious." I introduced myself and she welcomed me into her home to meet her parents, Michael and Josephine Saulle. We sat down in the kitchen and they invited me to share a glass of homemade red wine with them. It was just like the wine my Grandfather Giulio made when we lived in Brooklyn. I have to admit, they made me feel right at home. After a short time, Maria hinted we should get going, and so I politely thanked them for their hospitality.

I planned the first part of our date at Governor's Comedy Club in Levittown. We had reservations for a table but arrived a little later than I would've liked. The hostess seated us at a small round table for four. It was the last available table on the floor and the other two seats were still empty. The show hadn't begun yet, and we were talking and laughing like we knew each other for years. Out of the corner of my eye, I saw a couple walk into the room and head toward the last two seats in the house, which were at our tiny table. Normally that wouldn't be a problem because I enjoy meeting new people. But I knew this couple and my heart began to race as I became filled with anxiety. Maria saw the change in my demeanor as I became quiet. She asked what was wrong, but there was no time to tell her as they approached our table.

The couple began to greet us as they sat down, but as the woman recognized me as her sister's former fiancée, she choked on her greeting. Her husband handled the situation with a much lighter heart as he greeted me with a handshake and a smile. Still, I couldn't help but to feel uncomfortable and I knew Maria understood that something was wrong. I was admittedly in some distress over the circumstances and considered my options.

At that moment, Maria placed her right hand on top of my left and something remarkable happened. I had an unmistakable and overwhelming feeling, the likes of which I'd only experienced in the moment when Our Lady of Mercy placed her hand on my shoulder. Maria's single touch conveyed those same intense feelings of complete peace and perfect love, which Mother Mary shared with me as I floated out of my physical body and journeyed to Heaven. So in an instant, my feeling of distress melted away into peace, and I knew that Our Lady was telling me something special was happening.

We all became distracted as the show was beginning to start. Maria already knew that I had been engaged to be married and that it turned out badly. So during the show I told her who the couple was. She could hardly believe the odds that my x-fiancée's family sat with us on our first date. I honestly couldn't believe it either. Maria was so sensitive to my feelings and said she wouldn't mind if we missed the show, if it would make me feel more comfortable. I thought wow; she barely knows me and already is considerate of my feelings. I told her I wasn't going to let anything interfere with our first date, so we stayed and had a great time.

Nevertheless, I had to wonder how and why they came to be at our table on that particular day and at that specific moment. I hadn't seen them since I broke off the engagement, and I never saw them again. Remember, I don't believe at all, in coincidence. Also, as much as I believe in an inherently benevolent God, I also believe that there exists a malevolent power, which attempts to manipulate our relationship with God. I believe that they were unwitting pawns manipulated by a malevolent force to portray the most arduous circumstances upon us at our weakest moment.

Yet, I am sure that Our Lady of Mercy was standing right next to me as She made Her presence known when I needed Her most. I knew the moment Maria touched my hand that Our Lady was blessing our lives together. Of course, I didn't tell Maria that at the time. I continue to thank Jesus and Our Lady of Mercy for letting me know that I'm never alone.

After the show we drove to another club and spent the night dancing and talking. Everything about Maria was different from every other woman I'd ever met. Talking and listening to her was effortless. Holding her hand felt as natural as a morning sunrise, looking into her eyes felt like we'd known each other for a thousand years. Later, I drove her home, stole a first kiss, and wished her good night. As I drove to my home in Massapequa, I was sure that something special was beginning to happen. The next five months was a whirlwind romance for both of us. We spent most of our free time together laughing, dancing, and eating at great restaurants. As each new day passed, Maria continued to captivate me. We were in love and it felt amazing.

On April 9th, 160 days after we first met, I brought Maria up to my cabin on Deer Lake in Windsor, NY to ask for her hand in marriage. Earlier that week I respectfully declared my intentions to her parents. I planned to take her for a romantic ride in a rowboat, but when we pulled off the main road, I looked to my right expecting to see a lake full of water. Instead, I found a lake full of ice! I missed the thaw by a few weeks, but this little glitch wasn't going to hamper our plans.

We opened the cabin and I lit a fire in the wood burning stove. I was wearing a warm plaid jacket and the engagement ring was in the top pocket. I don't know what possessed me to take my jacket off and hang it on a kitchen chair, but I did. I went to switch on the circuit breaker, and when I came back I nearly had a heart attack when I saw Maria wearing my plaid jacket with the ring in it!

She was understandably cold and was only trying to stay warm. I was now noticeably freaking out a little and Maria thought I was either insane or rude when I insisted that she take the jacket off. I just needed to retrieve the ring and then I wrapped the jacket around her shoulders. I think she began to suspect something was up, because I saw her feeling the pockets in my jacket.

After we warmed up, I suggested we take a walk down by the lake. Frozen and all, it was still a beautiful sight. I thought it was all smooth sailing from here, but as we left the cabin a friendly dog named Tigra greeted us. Her name's Tigra because she's golden brown with black stripes. I'd known Tigra for years as a gentle and friendly companion. She's a Pit Bull mix with only three legs. She lost one of her front legs in a hunting accident. Still, it didn't slow her down.

So Maria and I walked down to the edge of Deer Lake for a romantic interlude followed closely behind by our three legged friend, who was looking for her own affection from me. Tigra was a great dog to play with, but not when I was trying to get engaged. I tried repeatedly to distract Tigra by throwing progressively larger and larger sticks for her to retrieve. Each time, without fail, she brought them back. This wasn't going exactly as I planned. I needed more time alone with Maria to ask her the most important question of our lives.

I thought I could slow Tigra down by throwing one of her

favorite things to fetch, rocks! All the while, Maria was laughing and apparently very amused at this dog's talents. I began to pick up progressively larger and larger rocks from the shoreline and throw them as far as I could. The last one was a small boulder and weighed about ten pounds. She chased it down, flipped it over and somehow opened her mouth wide enough to grab the rock. By the time I got down on one knee to propose to Maria, Tigra was there and dropped the ten ponder on the ground by her feet, wagging tail and all.

Tigra wasn't going anywhere so she watched us curiously as I told Maria that I wanted her to be in my life forever and ask her if she'd honor me by becoming my wife. Maria said yes and accepted the diamond engagement ring as her own. In retrospect, Tigra made our engagement even more memorable than I could've imagined and I'm glad the ice was frozen. It's funny how things happen for a reason.

Maria and I walked along the icy shore for a while and then went back to the cabin to warm up. Then I presented Maria with the following letter written 144 days earlier, but only delivered on the day she accepted my marriage proposal.

November 17, 1991

Dear Maria,

This fine day is complete and shortly I'll call you in anticipation of the rapture that is your voice. For when tomorrow arrives, I'll depart on a trip for a few days. Many times in the past when I've been alone upstate in my house, I'd feel forlorn. Thinking about it, I believe I won't feel that way this time. Even though I'll be by myself, you'll be in my mind and in my heart.

You don't know this now and I know it scares you a little when I talk like this since we only just met. But I know in my Heart and in my Soul that one day you'll be my one and only Bride. After we first met, each time I'd close my eyes and think of you, your beauteous image would appear to me covered by a white veil. By the time you read this we'll be engaged.

With all my Love,

Your Future Husband, Rob

On October 16th 1993, I married the woman of my dreams at Notre Dame Roman Catholic Church in New Hyde Park, where she grew up. When Father Gress pronounced us married, and we kissed for the first time as husband and wife, I knew that God and Our Lady of Mercy brought us together. It was the happiest day of our lives. Since then, my love for her has only grown, and she remains the greatest treasure of my life. Maria and I just celebrated our 20th wedding anniversary, and I'd like to share with you the card I wrote to her.

Dear Maria,

Thank you for teaching me how to love and for allowing me to love you all these years. Thank you for showing me a tender kind of love.

- ♥ A love that's soft yet strong enough to weather the storms.
- ♥ A love that's spontaneous yet enduring through the years.
- ♥ A love that grows us together and not apart.

- ♥ A love that's passionate even when you're exhausted.
- ♥ A love filled with happiness amidst the hectic days.
- ♥ A love so unyielding, it could only be a gift from Heaven.

And so after twenty years of Holy Matrimony, I re-pledge to you my whole life and all my love. I promise to love, honor and cherish you for all the days of my life. You're my Queen, my Angel, & my Wife, and you've given us three wonderful children. Thank you for sharing the last twenty years of your life with me and for always being beside me. I'll always continue to treasure each day we have together, even if it's filled with vacuuming and washing the dishes. The bond that we've made is a priceless treasure that can never be broken.

I'll Love You FOREVER
HAPPY 20TH ANNIVERSARY

Love, Rob

For years now I have used the symbol of angel wings on everything I give to Maria, because she knows I believe she's heaven sent. She's always kept us steady, grounded, and focused on the joy of life that's right in front of us. Our future is an integral part of our lives, and I'm not suggesting that you ignore it. I'm saying not to force it. My revelation about living one day at a time is that the future will unfold naturally and on its own.

In Maria's own delicate ways, she reminds me that, *Our only true future is today. The past is gone forever, and tomorrow may never come, so pay attention to today and enjoy it.* She's taught me how to live life one day at a time, and she's shown me how it's a much more fulfilling way of life. So I invite you practice paying more attention to what's in front of you rather than always gazing at your horizons, because I know you too deserve to live a richer life.

Chapter Eight

UNCOMMON EVENTS THAT SHAPED MY FAITH

D o you remember the days before the events that changed our lives forever? We had big plans and dreams for the future, until a living nightmare inverted our path. Today however, we can use our special gift of Survivor's Perspective to rewrite our dreams and our future one moment at a time. The truth is, we will never be the same again as we were before. Please don't misunderstand, I mean we will definitely be different yet much better than we were. I know this suggestion can be difficult to understand, especially when our minds constantly remind us of the anguish we endured.

I promise that your feelings of anger will convert to an empowering enlightenment, fueled by the knowledge that God has also called you. I know you think you own your anger and that it helps to make you stronger. I also know you believe you rule your anger and that it doesn't control you. I know you believe this because I used to believe it myself, but now I know better.

So to my fellow survivors, I'd like to offer you a testament of my faith in God. I offer you this opportunity to find new faith or to renew your faith in God. Believe me; God wants to help us each and every day. Yet, how can we connect with Him unless we believe that He loves us? I believe God loves us all, and that He's waiting for us to open the door and let him into our daily lives. I talk to God and to Our Lady of Mercy every day. I thank them for all that I am and for each new day. I promise to walk the path they put before me, wherever it leads. I tell them whatever is on my mind, and ask them to continue to support me each and every day. I would like to share with you two prayers I wrote in honor of Our Lord Jesus Christ and Our Blessed Lady of Mercy.

Thank You Lord

Thank you Lord for all that is wonderful and all that is dreadful. I've always known you were with me, and in my dire time you sent Our Lady to my aid. She filled me with your glorious light and sent me on my way.

I promise to strive each day, with humility and integrity, to use the gift I received for righteousness. With each passing day, my faith and love for you my God, grow ever stronger. I love You now and forever. Amen.

From the Arms of an Angel

From the arms of an angel,
With a gift in my soul.

Sent back with a message,
For all to be heard.

That peace will be given,
To those who deserve.

So believe in the Lord and
Forgive those who've wronged.

My purpose is clear,
And my faith is strong.

So believe in these words,
And with God you'll belong.

I've never felt alone, even when I was all by myself. I learned from a young age that I could talk to God and I knew He was always listening to me. I don't know how to explain how I knew, other than to say I felt his presence. But a relationship doesn't work, if only one of us does all the talking or the listening. Now this is where you have to really pay attention. I'd always try to listen to what God was saying to me. I wasn't listening for the actual sound of a voice but more for the thoughts and feelings He'd send me. This feeling is called many things such as; intuition, instinct, insight, and sixth sense. We all experience it and we can't always explain it. It happens to us so often in fact that we don't even consider what it is anymore.

Well, it's God communicating with us, so listen up. He always communicates with us, but if we're not listening, then how can we hear Him? It's widely believed that God's angels frequently send us messages in many forms, including; intuition, inspiration and through the use of numbers. My personal journey in search of understanding and enlightenment spanned more than twenty years, since the 29th day in the 11th month of 1990.

I've since come to understand that this particular day holds special meaning, because it's the 333rd day of our Gregorian calendar and the 3rd day of the 3rd month of the Hebrew calendar. In the entire universe there's one constant, one universal language, numbers. Number patterns exist and perpetuate themselves all around us. I believe the number 333 is a sign of the Holy Trinity and of Jesus Christ. I believe the most holy spirits are guiding me to achieve the goal they meant for me to carry out. I believe God called me to change to world, one day and one person at a time. I also believe the same is true of you. What do you think?

Since I met Mother Mary in Heaven, I knew that my future life had greater meaning. I thought what better way of emphasizing that, than a heavenly plan to meet Her on the 333rd day of the year. So is it significant that I died and met Our Lady on that particular day? I believe it is. I believe it is destiny. I am just an ordinary man who's had some extraordinary experiences. While I have learned a great deal from my experiences, I'm no more special than you are. I believe each of us has a greater purpose, part of which should be to give something back to those who need it more than we do.

Twisted anger filled me up for many years. My rage against my unknown assailant clouded my judgment and obscured my path. But over time, and through listening and praying to

Mother Mary and Jesus, I have been able to put true forgiveness in my heart. My mission to teach other survivors only begins with this book. It is my hope each of you will surrender your anger to find enlightenment and later teach others to do the same.

I believe with all my heart that God has a plan for you. He tries to share himself with each of us, every single day. All we have to do is hear Him, in our minds and in our hearts. Can you hear Him? Do you believe in Him? If you already believe in God then you are on the right path. Next, establish a rapport with God. Yes, I mean try talking to God. Yeah, just like you talk to a friend, say what you're feeling out loud. I promise He will hear you.

You know that God is real, but do you listen to him when he speaks to you? Don't dismiss this question as folly, because it may be the most important question of your entire life. I know it is for me. So, do you listen to God when he speaks to you? You may not be so fortunate to actually hear the words of God with you own ears, however, He sends his messages to us in many ways. All we have to do is listen with our thoughts and feelings. Every one of us is a vessel containing the spirit of God, and He uses our spirit to guide us to do his righteous work. Always remember that He only wants good for us, and for us to do good for others. Here is one true story of how I listened to His message, and changed the life of a young man named Joe.

Faith Re-Gained

It was the evening of Sunday, December 14th 1997. Maria and I had plans to leave North Shore University Hospital in Manhasset the next morning with our first-born child, Adam. It was about time for dinner and Maria was content with the hospital meal. Suddenly, I had an overwhelming felling that I needed to go to Vincent's Clam Bar for Italian food to take back to the hospital. Maria felt it was too far away since so many good Italian restaurants were closer. She was right. It would take at least thirty minutes of drive time from Manhasset to Carle Place and back on a Sunday night, not including the time to order and wait for the food. So round trip, probably about an hour total. Yet I continued to have an irresistible need to journey to this specific restaurant, but I didn't know why at the time.

When I arrived, I ordered mussels marinara for Maria and manicotti for myself. Then I sat at the bar and waited. It was a busy night in the restaurant, but oddly there was scarcely anyone at the bar. I ordered a cognac from the bartender and when he brought my drink, I greeted him with a "how ya doing". But instead of giving me the expected 'I'm good', he look at me strangely as if he'd known me all his life. And then he said, "I feel like my life is over. I'm going to kill myself tonight; I just don't know how I'm going to do it yet." I paused long enough to compose myself following his remarkable statement, until I realized that he was deadly serious.

There are moments in our lives when we're given opportunities to make a difference. It's in these moments that we can change the world, one individual at a time. Blessed with a second chance at life and given the mandate to work in His name, I knew this was my opportunity. As he momentarily stepped away to help an approaching customer, I knew it was my responsibility to save him from certain death.

When he returned, I asked him to tell me what was troubling him. He introduced himself as Joe. He looked like he was in his early twenties, and explained to me how his whole life had come unraveled. He told me about his girlfriend named Maryann, of more than two years and how she had recently left him for another guy. In the course, she took all the money he saved up and was planning on using to buy her an engagement ring. I could see the heart-broken devastation in his eyes. She had crushed his spirit into a fine powder and callously strewn it into the harsh wind.

He explained that when she left him, he became drunk and wrecked his car after crashing it into a tree. But with no money, he couldn't buy a replacement. Miraculously, he walked away from this crash with only a scratch. I couldn't help wondering if this was an accident at all, or rather his first attempt at suicide. After losing the love of his life, his spirit to live, all his money, and his car; fate dealt him another blow. He lost full-time job as Assistant Manager at a supermarket and his apartment for failure to pay rent.

Joe also told me that his parents divorced when he was twelve years old and that he had little contact with them. With no place to live, he moved in with a friend and just started working as a bartender at the restaurant part-time and for minimum wage. Joe told me he was looking forward to death because it would end his emotional pain and agony. When I told him I understood what he was feeling and that death wouldn't solve his problems, he replied with arrogance, "How could you know?"

I began by recounting the feelings of lost love which I once had as a much younger man, and remembered how those feelings led to my own thoughts of suicide. I told Joe that during this time in my life, I also felt as though my life had no purpose, and that I might be better-off dead. I told Joe that after the long period of feeling sorry for myself, I reached out to God for help. With each new day, I began to pray for guidance, support, and wisdom. I completely opened myself to God and asked him to fill me up. From that time and every day since, I've felt that God's been constantly with me, guiding me through life. I told Joe I'd learned that *"Life isn't about us; it's about God and what He can do through us."*

Then I explained to Joe how I died in a shooting seven years earlier. Intent on capturing every word, Joe listened as I described the journey out of my physical body and to another place that was nothing like where we live. I told him when I arrived in Heaven, how Our Lady of Mercy gave me a precious gift. I explained to Joe, that Mother Mary told me I wasn't ready to join her in Heaven and that I had to live to fulfill a destiny. I explained further how we're all born with a piece of God inside of us and that this innate potential enables us to accomplish great feats of humanity. Our constraint however, is that our lives are so consumed by inanimate objects and that we fail to act on the signs that we constantly receive from the angels all around us.

Joe listened intently as I described the unbearable physical and emotional pain I endured day after day. The expression in his eyes was like that of a lost soul, clamoring for someone to save him. He bought me a drink, and asked me to continue. I told him about the day when I could endure no further agony, and shouted loudly and asked God to end my pain. I recounted my experience of how the voice of God responded to my cry for relief. I told Joe how I heard the voice clearly as it said, *"If you want an end to all of your pain, simply let go of your will to live and you will be released. Give up and you will come Home. The choice is yours."* I explained to Joe that while Heaven is the Most Glorious Place, I made a conscious decision to live and endure to pain, knowing that there was something more to live for. God was with me. I told Joe that God was also with him, and all he had to do was to open his heart to realize it.

When I finished, Joe spoke the words that I'll never forget. He said, *"The reason you had to come here tonight wasn't for good food, it was for me. Tonight you gave me something I lost long ago, faith. You saved my life and I'll always remember you as my angel sent from God."* I was overcome with tears of joy from his revelation. I thanked Joe for the drink and asked him to listen with his mind and his heart for the signs that God would surely send him, to live and help others. I returned to Maria at the hospital and when I shared my story with her, she realized why I needed to travel so far for food that night.

Two weeks later I returned to Vincent's Restaurant for some take-out on my way home from my office in Garden City. I ordered my food at the counter and walked toward the bar in hopes of seeing Joe. I made my way through the crowd of customers and saw him working behind the bar. When Joe looked up and saw me, I could see how filled he was with happiness and a new purpose. As he gave me a pronounced thumbs-up, I knew that he'd be okay.

Providence Lends a Hand

When I was seventeen years old and living in Farmingdale, I barely escaped from an exploding fireball. There were a group of teenage boys causing trouble in our quiet suburban neighborhood. They were harassing some of the younger kids on my block, and one of my neighbors complained to me that these kids were walking through their property carrying lumber. I knew they were hanging out in the local woods by my house and that they must've built a fort. So, like the Good Samaritan, I went into the woods with two of my friends, John Hasley and Jason Winters, to find and destroy their hideout.

The woods were thick with trees, brush and thorn bushes. We searched up and down looking for a structure, but found nothing. We knew it must be here so we looked for anything out of the ordinary. Then I noticed a bunch of dead bushes and tree branches. We made our way over and found that it was camouflage for an underground cave-fort. We couldn't believe our eyes. We've seen above ground forts in the woods before, but never had anyone conceived digging a cave! Underneath the dead tree branches and bushes we found a 4 by 8 foot piece of plywood. John and Jason removed the wood to expose a nearly four foot square hole in the earth that descended about seven feet deep.

One of us had to go in and check it out, so I volunteered. I know it was a bad idea, but I did it anyway. The first thing I remember was the smell of musty dirt. Even though it was summer time, it was so much cooler underground. The vertical drop turned into a six foot long horizontal tunnel that opened into a ten foot square room. It was high enough to stand in and in the middle of it there was a couch. Yes, a couch. The tunnel and the room had a frame of 2 by 4 inch beams and plywood to support the ceiling from collapsing.

The question was how do we destroy an underground fort? Well, with fire of course. We figured the wood and couch would burn with a little help from some gasoline and after it was over, these troublemakers wouldn't return to bother anyone. So since it was my bright idea, or not so much bright as dimly lit, I volunteered to go back in the hole and burn it down. I soaked the couch and wood frames with gas, and walked down the tunnel towards the entrance. I remember how smart I felt just before I struck the match. I certainly didn't expect what happened next.

When I threw the lit match onto the couch, the gas fumes in the tunnel ignited as a ball of fire consumed everything in its path, and I was in its path. I never expected it to happen so quickly. My heart was pounding as I ran franticly toward to opening. I'll never forget the high pitched screaming sound the hellish flames made as they roared toward my tender flesh. There was no way at all I could make a vertical leap of more than seven feet and clear the hole without serious injury, but I was going to try. I jumped as high as I could with my arms stretched out above my head, like something magical was going to happen to save me.

As I jumped up, John and Jason happened to be in perfect position to grab each of my arms and pull me clear out of the hole. Just as my feet came out, I turned my body and saw this fire ball from hell rise several feet above the ground. Horrified at what had just happened and yet relieved at the outcome, the three of us sat motionless in the woods as smoke began to bellow from the hole. The timing of the rescue by my two friends was more than spectacular, it was purely divine.

I've no doubt that God was instrumental that day in guiding John and Jason to save my life. Look at it from my perspective. How else could my completely unplanned rescue, have been so perfectly timed and executed by a couple of teenagers. Was it sheer luck, or divine guidance? I know exactly what it was and I thank God for helping John and Jason to save me that day.

Angels Riding Shotgun

When I was eighteen years old, my friends and I barely escaped certain death from a near car crash. I was driving upstate NY with my two best friends, Mike Doner and Ron Duswalt, to our cabin on Deer Lake in the town of Windsor. We were driving in my 1977 Camaro Z28. Ron was in the back and Mike was up front. It was late afternoon on a Friday and we were on the Palisades Parkway, a route that we'd taken many times before. The two-lane was wide open. Out of my side window I could see the grassy median, which was about forty yards wide, separating us from cars moving in the other direction.

When you've driven the same route over and over, you tend to form habits. Well, we always stuck to the fast lane, even if there was no one else on the road. We were in the mountains, so the roadway would peak at the top of a hill and then go down for a while before heading up again. Seconds before we reached the top of a steep hill I had the overwhelming urge to switch into the right lane, so I moved over.

Just as we crested the hill, and before Mike and I even had time to gasp, another car driving in the wrong direction blew by us in the lane we were just in. He was driving eastbound in the westbound fast lane. He must've driven onto the highway from an exit ramp. Remember, even though we were wearing our seat belts, cars from the '70's didn't have safety features like air bags. The only reason Mike, Ron and I didn't die that day in a mangled car crash is because I listened to the message I heard from the angels to, "Get out of the way".

After we sighed with relief, I remember Mike asking me why I moved over into the right lane for no apparent reason.

I told him because God gave me a message to change lanes. For me, there's no doubt that God saved us that day. Imagine what would've happened if I wasn't listening? Are you listening, can you hear Him?

The Funeral March Plays

In 1983, on a Sunday afternoon in the summer of my twentieth year, I was driving my Z28 slowly down the street of my good friend Eddie. We'd just finished rebuilding his girl friend Patty's straight six-cylinder engine a few days before, and I wanted to see how it was running.

My right hand was on the steering wheel. I had my driver's window rolled down and my left arm hanging slightly out of it. I had a musical juke box in the car connected to a speaker under the hood. It was a cool toy that I used often, and it played short bursts of ninety-nine different songs. To play a song, I had to press the number on the keypad and then press enter.

As I approached Eddie's house, my musical horn played a song all by itself. My hands were nowhere near the buttons on the keypad, as it played the eleven unmistakable notes of the Funeral March! I was admittedly a little shocked as I stopped the car and looked around for anyone in the street, thinking it was someone's idea of a practical joke. But there was no one. I parked the car, got out, and told Eddie what just happened. We finally agreed it must've been an electrical short circuit, and dismissed it. Yet, of all the ninety nine songs to short circuit to, why did it play the Funeral March?

I woke up the next morning and drove to Hofstra University in Uniondale, where I was studying Finance and Banking. It's about a thirteen mile drive each way, nine miles of which is on the parkway. After my classes finished I drove home, changed into a suit and drove a couple of miles to work at the Sunrise Mall branch of The Dime Savings Bank of New York. After I finished working for the day I got into my car and drove home. I pulled into the driveway, put the car into park and shut the engine. Just then, I heard the screeching sounds of twisting metal coming from the front end of my car. A few seconds later, the passenger side front wheel of my Camaro broke completely off and the front end of the car came crashing onto the driveway!

I was still sitting in the driver's seat as panic came over me. I got out of the car to see the wheel several feet away from my Camaro. I remember thinking how my horn had spontaneously played the Funeral March the day before and how fortunate I was not to be driving on the highway when it happened. So, do you think the horn played the Funeral March all by itself, or was it the act of an Angel warning me of impending doom? Do you think it was coincidence the car fell apart only after I finished driving thirty miles that day?

There's absolutely no doubt in my mind and in my heart that Angels were trying to warn me the day before by playing that fateful song. I believe God intervened and saved me that day by waiting for me to be safe before the car collapsed. I've often thought about the potential calamity caused if I was traveling on the parkway when the front wheel snapped off. So each day of my life I thank God for protecting and watching over me.

Are you listening to the messages God is sending you? Can you hear them in your mind and in your heart? I'm certain He's trying to communicate with us and that He hears us when we speak to Him. Many of you already know what I mean. You understand that by asking God to be part of our lives and fill our souls with His love, that only great things will be the result.

When I pray to God and ask Him to be part of me, I can feel a great warmth come over me. It's like a warm blanket of love which fills up my body. I can feel His peace and comfort flow into and through my body, washing away all of my dread.

Believe me, once you've experienced these gifts that only the Lord himself can bestow, you'll become a better, wiser, stronger, and more forgiving person than you could've ever imagined. You'll look on events all around you with a renewed and glorious perspective.

Chapter Nine

ONE PARTICULAR MIDNIGHT
THE DREAMS THAT SHAPE MY PERSONAL HELL

For me, the worst of it are my nights, for my nights rule my days. Lying there barely asleep, my mind is ruled by a constant battle of pain, fear, blood, and always my inevitable death. The constant nightmares of my death have come in every manner imaginable. The old standard is death by gun at the hands of The Olive Skinned Man. But I'm also accustomed to death by knife, drowning, torture, and zombies as well as by a supernatural evil which dismembers my body limb from limb.

At times the nightmares of my death are swift, but usually they're torturously slow and drawn out. In the end I wake up screaming on the outside and trembling for my life on the inside. My horrible nights seem filled with a constant battle for my physical well being and my life. But it's not like I'm looking for a fight, but rather fights and death are looking for me, and they always know where to find me.

Everyone has bad dreams, even nightmares from time to time. But for those of us suffering day to day from the effects of

Trauma Induced Stress, it's unlike anything you could imagine. Each night I must face a never ending struggle to stay alive. The face of my enemy takes on many shapes from human to shades of evil figures. Many of my nightmares repeat over and over and year after year. Sometimes I'm actively fighting for my life and other times I'm paralyzed and can't move or scream.

The venue changes from the bank where it first began, to an unforgiving city, a bloody beach, and even into my own home where I've witnessed my own children's murders. The feeling of pain and loss is bad enough when I die in my sleep, but believe me, it's far worse to experience the nightmare murder of my own children. Even seeing them and hugging them the next morning isn't enough to shake the traumatic feeling of their death, which lasts sometimes for days.

Each night before bedtime my anxiety builds, knowing my fate will be horrific, and each morning I feel physically and mentally traumatized from the very tangible physical and neurochemical affects. For years, family and friends have tried to understand how my nightmares of blood, gore and death so dramatically and negatively affect my days. Yet, they can't understand because when they have bad dreams, they feel fine the next day. I feel, as many of you do, that our family and friends may be unaware they're in fact minimizing the legitimate physical, mental, and emotional effects of these recurring and traumatizing nightmares. Before I discuss the effects of my nightmares, I'd first like to share with you some of *The Dreams that Shape My Personal Hell.*

The Place it All Began

On one particular midnight, I found myself once more as a Bank Manager. I open the doors as usual at 9 a.m. and organize my staff for the day's work. Everything seems in place when an Olive Skinned Man walks ominously through the doorway. His body's shrouded by a frigid mist which feeds on the life force of every living thing. I can only watch helplessly as the frigid mist spreads out and darkens the room. I feel paralyzed to move as he draws nearer.

The Olive Skinned Man reveals a gun and points it straight at me. I can see the evil in his eyes, like a painting on the wall. The painting depicts a tortured man, corrupted by sin and motivated by greed. I'm frozen with terror and I can see directly down the barrel of his weapon as bullets repeatedly explode out of the gun and shred my flesh. My own warm blood running down onto my skin signals his victory is nearly complete. The Olive Skinned Man grins with contentment, but the job isn't over yet.

I struggle in vain to fight back as I collapse onto the bank floor. He stands over me smiling as if receiving a rewarded in some cruel way. Then he leans over my languishing body and plunges his left hand straight into my chest, tearing out my heart. Cold and alone, my blood explodes across the room. The Olive Skinned Man stands up with my still beating heart in his hand and begins to walk away. I see yet more blood oozing out of my disconnected heart as he squeezes it tighter and tighter, until it dries up and turns to ashes. Then the Olive Skinned Man waits until my death is complete, but only to return again and again.

The Unforgiving City

On one particular midnight, I was on my own once again in the Unforgiving City. My heart was pounding so fast and so hard it nearly tore a channel straight through my chest. Breathless, I continued to run at my ultimate limit, as I heard the gunshots right behind me and knew death was nearby.

A hard rain just finished as steam rose from the hot blacktop. The streets, littered with puddles of murky doom around every corner, felt alive with deceit. As each warm breath condensed in the chilly night air, I became weaker and weaker. I stopped for only a second and a bullet smacked through my left arm. I ran down an alley and slipped through an unlocked door into an apartment where I thought I'd be safe, for at least a moment.

I avoided the elevator, to not leave an audible or visual trace of my whereabouts. I ran up four flights of stairs and hid in a utility closet. My adrenaline filled veins blocked the pain from the gunshot wound. I grabbed a towel from the shelf and ripped it into a strip. Then I tied it tightly on my arm just above the wound to slow the bleeding. I thought I just might make it out alive. Maybe they wouldn't find me in here.

Suddenly, I panicked when the stairwell door at the end of the corridor opened and several angry men began unloading their weapons. Multiple shots rang out and tore easily through the walls. I don't know how they found me, but I had to keep moving. If only I had a gun, then I could at least fight back. As I opened the door to escape, I could see the frenzy of rage that poured out through their eyes and fueled their bloodlust. I didn't know why, I only knew they needed to kill me in a very brutal manner.

With all my strength, I busted straight through the closest

door and crashed through a window, and onto the fire escape. There was a group on the street firing at me, so I headed to the roof. Halfway up the first flight I slipped on the metal stairs and fell backward. I crashed hard, back onto the fourth floor landing, cracking the back of my head on the cold steel and giving up precious seconds. I got back on my feet still dazed by the blow as one of them came out from the window and grabbed me. He held me by the shirt with his left hand, and in the other he held a .357 Magnum revolver. I looked up to view his face, and it was him. It was the same Olive Skinned Man from that fateful day, whose eyes gleamed with the identical dread horror and carnal blood lust.

It was time to do or die. So I grabbed his head with both hands and plunged my thumbs deep into his eyes, blinding him and giving back some of the pain, which I was now beginning to feel. It didn't even faze me when the putrid opaque fluid from his eye sockets gushed out of his head and onto my hands. In one motion, I took the revolver out of his right hand and tossed him over the fourth floor railing and onto the street below. Finally, I achieved a modicum of success, one down and a small army to go.

I moved as fast as I could up the next three floors and to the roof. I quickly checked the gun. It was a sturdy .357 Magnum with a stainless finish, and I knew it had the stopping power to put any man down. But as I touched the frigid gunmetal, its evil ran through my fingertips and into my arms. This gun came from a killer and his evil ran through it. Even out of his hands, it was still trying to kill me, so I threw it high into the air and watched it crumble into an ominous mist. I had no plan other than to keep moving forward. I didn't know how I could defeat an evil army; I only knew I had to survive as long as I could.

I was weak from exhaustion and trapped on the roof with nowhere to run. The smell of my blood wafted in the air through the red soaked strip of towel bound to my arm. At once, dozens with a singular intent surrounded me. Then I tried to charge the roofs edge and jump to the next building, as a hail of lead enveloped me. As I neared the roofs edge, my body literally imploded from the gunfire, and my corpse fell seven stories into the darkness.

Close to Home

On one particular midnight I found myself at home with my Daughter, Jessica. It was the middle of the afternoon and we were in the kitchen fixing lunch. I was making a ham and Munster with mayo on an English muffin, and Jessica was preparing her favorite hazelnut chocolate spread on toasted wheat bread. We were home alone but suddenly interrupted by the sound of screeching tires coming from the street.

We went by the front window to check it out and saw three men inside an old brown car. Before we knew what was going on, they pointed guns at us and began to fire repeatedly. Their bullets tore easily through the wall and shattered the bay window into a thousand flying pieces of glass. I immediately grabbed Jessica pushing her to the floor and jumped on top of her to shield her body from the deadly projectiles. When the torrent was over and their car raced away, I uncovered Jessica to reveal her lifeless body lying in a puddle of her own fresh warm blood.

I tried as hard as I could to save her, but it was no use. Jessica was dead. My emotions sank into oblivion. It felt like my heart tore straight out of my chest. My face soaked with tears and my hands with blood, I reached into my pocket for a phone and called Maria. When she answered, I could barely speak the words to tell her that our baby girl is dead. I could hear Maria's voice on the other end, but I just zoned out into my own despair.

I finally woke up from my nightmare at 3:30 a.m., drenched in my own sweat. My hands were shaking uncontrollably and tears were rolling down my face. I knew it was only a bad dream, but its effects weren't over. I struggled out of bed and up the stairs to see my Jessica, alive and well in her bed.

There she was sleeping safely, but in my heart she felt very much dead. I touched her beautiful warm face just to make sure and then I curled up on the floor next to her bed and stayed a while. I saw Jessica the next morning as she walked downstairs into the kitchen. I hugged her, still crying from the night before. My feeling of grief lasted for several days until subsiding.

Underworld

On one particular midnight I'm alone in complete pitch-black darkness. Strewn onto a cold and damp concrete floor, my naked body felt tormented. The setting seems foreign to me. I rise and begin walking through the blackness. Searching with outstretched arm, this place is devoid of the audible and the physical. It seems like I'm walking in virtual blindness for hours and hours.

Then with one last step, the floor beneath me ends, and I fall off. I fall, spin, and tumble for some time until I land into what feels like hundreds of frozen hands and fingers reaching out to grab me and pull me into the underworld. They're all over me and I can't escape them no matter how hard I struggle. As the hands pull me tighter and tighter, it feels like my limbs will tear clean off my body. Then when I've no more strength to fight, the hands pull me beneath them and into their world of torment.

Death on a Sunday Afternoon

On one particular midnight, I was standing outside my home on a sunny Sunday afternoon talking to my friend Ron. Just then, a truck with at least four men drove past and slowed down in front of the house just next door. I noticed through the open car windows that they had automatic machine guns. I told Ron it's a hit and to hide behind my truck parked in the street. The thugs got out of their truck and opened fire on my neighbor's house, showering it with hundreds of bullets. I could hear my neighbors screaming in the street as they ran for their lives. A couple came outside and quickly fell victim to the onslaught. I yelled to everyone to get back in their houses.

By this time the men surrounded me with guns and took me hostage. I went with them willingly to stop the senseless killing. As we drove away, I looked at my wife and children with a good-bye glance, possibly for the last time. I soon realized a connection to a million dollar robbery, as an armored car filled with cash drove closely behind us. Meanwhile, I was thinking of an escape plan and waiting for an opportunity to act. Unfortunately, I was sitting in the front passenger seat and the bandit sitting behind me had a gun aimed directly at the back of my head the entire time.

We stopped at several large warehouses three times as we headed west into New York City. I think they were meeting with other men who followed them into the city. It was still light out as they arrived at their final destination in front of another large warehouse. I knew we were near the waterfront because I could smell the salt air and fish. I also overheard the one giving orders say they were leaving on a boat.

A dozen other men with machine guns joined them. Then they all began firing hundreds of bullets into the air in excitement of a successful heist. I thought, wouldn't someone hear these gunshots? Where are the police? They acted like they weren't afraid of the police, like they owned the entire city! Yet I remained hopeful in an apparently hopeless situation. Finally, they removed me from the truck and shot me in the back of my head. I could feel my head exploding as I died on a Sunday afternoon. I never had a chance.

The Three Faces of Death

Part One

On one particular midnight I found myself among those of my own kindred spirit. We were a Special Forces military unit patrolling and protecting an ocean beachfront and I was their commander. We were strong, well trained and armed only with long wooden staffs. The tide was out and there was barely a ripple on the surface of the water. It was evening and a cloud cover had moved in to dim the already scant moonlight. The sand beneath our boots was ivory white and the air was warm. It was shaping up to be an easy mission, forgetting for a moment there were no easy missions. I'd been on this beach many times before and it never ended well.

Suddenly, out of the depths of the murky black waters came a horde of pig-like soldiers so foul and horrid, they must've been demonic. They walked like men but appeared as swine, with pig like faces, and were also carrying wooden staffs. They had no boat or craft, but as if born directly from the frigid sea. Their numbers were many, and I quickly became separated from my unit.

The largest pig engaged me in combat, and as it drew closer, I could see its wet skin dripping with slimy ooze. As we began to battle, I was confident that I was the superior warrior. Blow after blow, I was faster and stronger than it was. I blocked a series of attacks from the swine and took to the counteroffensive. I pummeled the beast to the ground until it was dead and then watched it melt back into the depths from where it came. The result was the same for every member of my unit and it seemed that we were victorious.

Part Two

After this grueling battle with these formidable yet clearly weaker adversaries, my team and I began up the beach to our main camp. Then the setting changed. My team vanished and I felt alone. Now, instead of a wooden staff, I was now holding a dingy frying pan in my left hand from the meal we shared hours before. Then I noticed something else that wasn't there before, a mighty rushing river. The river ran along the shoreline until it became finally swallowed by the cold black sea. I stretched out my arm and dipped the dirty pan into the rushing waters to clean it off. I misjudged the power of the river and when the curve of the pan met the rushing rapids, I became sucked into the bone chilling waters.

I was out of control. I felt myself tumbling beneath the unstoppable power of the beast which had an agenda of its own. It was drawing me further and further out to sea. I couldn't swim up because the turbulent waters seemed stronger on the surface. But I had to at least try to react in some way, no matter how powerful this adversary was. I knew the only thing I could do was to swim down even deeper, hoping the waters were calmer there. So with every ounce of strength I had left from fighting this foe, I felt myself equalizing within the water. I'd made it out of the tumultuous river but my fate seemed even grimmer. I had no choice in the path I took, and now found myself drawn far out into the unforgiving sea.

The air was deep with blackness and the grip of the icy waters held me fast. I struggled to gain my bearing, but with no avail. The moon and stars had vanished. An impenetrable veil of clouds now obscured any glimmer of light from the shoreline. And all I could hear was the salty wash of the sea against my now frozen face. What use was being alive amid this vast foe if my path to survival was masked with misfortune?

I chose an arbitrary direction and then began to swim, knowing that without a point of view I'd likely end up swimming in circles. Time felt slower and each stroke diminished until I began to plummet below the surface. I saw a thousand arms and five thousand fingers from the deep reaching out to grasp my flesh, like hooks in a fish. I could feel the hands of death firmly holding on to my near dead body. I thought, "How could it end like this?" Then I felt my life slip away and I was dead.

Part Three

When I died, I became a spirit of my mortal self, floating inside a hospital room. The lifeless and sallow shell of my own flesh was lying dead on the bed below me, dressed in a hospital gown and surrounded by my grieving family. I could hear the agony in their voices as they wept saying "Did they find Rob yet?" And the reply, "No, Rob's lost and they can't find him."

The room became silent as the steady sound of heavy footsteps approached from the hallway outside the door. It sounded like heavy boots, 'heel-toe, heel-toe', and they were getting closer. I remember seeing my family's attention drawn away from my corpse and toward the door. The footsteps stopped as the gleaming brass knob began to turn.

The door cracked open and a brilliant light shown through. Standing there in the doorway was a third version of me, except he was very much alive. He looked strong and was wearing blue jeans, black work boots, and a black leather motorcycle jacket. He was focused and his actions were deliberate, as he moved closer to our lifeless shell lying on the bed. In a single movement he sat on the bed and laid down directly into our dead body, then vanished.

The strong version of us wearing the leather jacket was gone, but his consequential actions reanimated our dead body. Just like that I was alive once more, warm blood, pink skin and eyes wide open. My spirit's prevailing attraction to my physical body was also unmistakable, as I too joined together with my body. The last thing I remember was my brother Pete saying, "We found him!"

Chapter Ten

THE IMPACT OF NIGHTMARES

Like many of you survivors, the quality of my night's sleep rules the quality of my days. We don't dream like everyone else. The traumatic events we've experienced have somehow changed the way we dream. So here's what twenty three years of experience has taught me about chronic nightmares. Nightmares so powerful, that they literally transform how we feel, what we think, and who we are.

First, it's important to understand the differences between a normal human sleep cycle and the sleep cycle of an individual suffering from chronic Trauma Induced Stress. The purpose of normal sleep is as uncertain as it is complex. There are several stages in a healthy human sleep cycle. The most important of these stages is Rapid Eye Movement or REM. There seems to be a biological and a psychological need for REM sleep, although it's not really known why. A common belief is that our brains use REM sleep to process through our emotions in the form of dreams. A healthy REM sleep cycle normally occurs every 90 to 120 minutes, and lasts for about 20 to 40 minutes.

When we experience healthy REM sleep, we feel more rested and refreshed the next morning. It's known that healthy REM sleep has two phases: phasic and tonic. It's also known that when we experience healthy REM sleep, certain physiological events take place. In the phasic stage, our extremities may display slight twitching movements. However, during the tonic phase, our bodies experience selective sleep paralysis of the major muscles, or REM atonia. This perfectly normal part of healthy sleep allows our involuntary functions, like heart rate and breathing to continue. Simultaneously, it protects us from physically acting out in our dreams and injuring ourselves, and those sleeping beside us.

We're not sure exactly how the brain produces REM atonia. We do know that during this particular stage of sleep, the production in the brain of the chemical neurotransmitters histamine, serotonin, and norepinephrine are significantly reduced. These neurotransmitters are responsible for relaying chemical messages in the brain. It's believed these reduced levels of neurotransmitters are responsible for this selective paralysis of the large muscle groups.

Like many of you suffering from the effects of Trauma Induced Stress, I've been experiencing unhealthy sleep patterns for more than twenty years. I'm not a doctor, but what I have learned from my doctors and my experience has taught me volumes about the condition we face. I've spent two decades and tens of thousands of dollars on classical and holistic treatments, as well as prescription drugs. One of my goals was to learn the causes of horrific recurring nightmares, and how to quell them. So after more than twenty years, I finally have some answers and some well-deserved relief.

When we experience healthy REM sleep, the production in the brain of the chemical neurotransmitter norepinephrine is greatly reduced. But as I've learned from my doctors, this is usually not the case for those of us suffering from nightmares triggered by chronic Trauma Induced Stress. First, you need to understand that norepinephrine is not only a neurotransmitter; it's also a kind of hormone. Norepinephrine is like the hormone adrenaline, which we know supercharges us when we're frightened or excited. This is thought to be the reason our dreams aren't pleasant or even neutral, but rather always nightmares of blood, gore, and death.

Before I experienced Trauma Induced Stress and woke up from a bad dream, it was over. After returning to sleep, the bad dream didn't come back or continue. However, after my brutal shooting, near death, and 77 day stint in the hospital, nothing about my dreams was ever the same. I suspect that Trauma Induced Stress may also be turning your dreams into *fighting for your life* nightmares.

If you're like me, your nightmares don't end when you wake up from them. After we fall back asleep the nightmare either replays or simply continues from where it left off. I've gone so far as to get out of bed and watch TV or take a shower in the middle of the night. But no matter what I did to try and break the cycle of nightmares, they just kept rolling on. It's like my mind wasn't stopping the dream but only temporarily pressing the pause button, only to press play again when I fell back asleep. It's believed the unusually high levels of norepinephrine/adrenaline in the brain during the tonic stage of REM sleep may be responsible. This is why our brains don't cycle past the nightmares and why we're stuck in a bloody death loop that plays over and over.

While healthy sleep patterns induce REM atonia of the major muscles, those of us suffering from terrifying nightmares caused by Trauma Induced Stress aren't so fortunate. We lack this natural event, and we physically act out in our nightmares, putting ourselves and the ones we love in harm's way. I regret to say that over the years, my wife Maria has accidentally been on the receiving end of my punching and kicking during nightmares. This is an unacceptable problem that must be solved. We can no longer put our loved ones at risk, and I believe a solution is in sight.

Yet another complication of our adrenaline filled nightmares is, it makes us feel the physical and emotional pain of our terror for hours or even days after we wake up. It's believed that stress hormones, especially adrenaline, are the key to imprinting strong memories. That's why you remember so vividly, your wedding day, the first time you rode a bicycle, or closing that big deal at work. As well, it's also the reason you'll never forget every detail of the death of a loved one or a blow-out fight.

You can so easily remember exactly how you felt, what you saw around you, even what it smelt like. The amazing thing is, these memories stay with you forever and it's all because of adrenaline. The same belief is also true of our nightmares. When we dream with adrenaline filled nightmares, the emotional and physical response is so intense and vivid, that even in a wakeful state, we continue to feel the effects for hours and even days later.

Sometimes, the terror in my nightmares doesn't resign itself to killing just me. My nightmares have relentlessly horrified me by brutally slaying of each of my family members, including my wife Maria, and each of our three children. Please understand that after a survivor wakes from dreaming such atrocities, the feelings of deep emotional loss of a loved one can stay with us for days. My most recent nightmare of this nature involved the shooting death of my daughter Jessica. When she died in my arms, I was helpless to save her. I remember waking up from it and continuing to feel all the visceral emotions of her loss. When I saw her the next morning, I hugged her again and again.

The memory of her death in my nightmare was so filled with norepinephrine; it felt as real to me as if she'd actually died. So for the next two days I felt and acted as if she was gone, even though she was right in front of me. All of this caused because my supercharged nightmare was full of this powerful stress hormone, norepinephrine. Yet, amid this seeming never-ending torture we barely endure for years, there exists a bastion of hope.

Since my nightmares of death have plagued me, I've searched for any relief I could find. Keep in mind that our nights rule our days. So when we experience chronic nightmares of dying, it can inhibit our minds from functioning rationally and calmly in a waking state. We become unable to cope with even the smallest stressors. Every sound and voice becomes magnified many times over, forcing us to retreat to the quietest room in the house. Every simple task triggers mental confusion and frustration as well as physical shaking and elevated heart rate and breathing. In short, we feel useless.

Over the years, many doctors treated me for this stress related condition, including the symptoms of nightmares, but with little success. However, several years ago I met Dr. Jack Katz, an experienced psychiatrist specializing in anxiety conditions, and my symptoms began to change for the better. He understood that many of the drugs other doctors prescribed for me only made my symptoms worse in the long run. His approach was gentler and less experimental. For the first time, I felt I was in the right place. As it turns out, I was.

Dr. Katz has regularly treated me for seven years now. With each new year it feels like small parts of the 'old Rob' are coming back. Most importantly, it's easier for me to laugh and to enjoy my family again. While Dr. Katz is still uncertain when I'll be able to return to work for The Bank, he's proven to be an invaluable resource in my challenge against this worthy adversary.

In August of 2011, Dr. Katz suggested that I consider taking a prescription drug which has proved to reduce the frequency and magnitude of chronic nightmares for individuals suffering from this trauma condition. Dr. Katz understood my conservative philosophy on taking any drugs, let alone more drugs. But he suggested that if this drug could ease my nightmares, I might be able to reduce my other nighttime medications. I thought that sounded like a good plan.

Dr. Katz described the drug as an older high blood pressure medication, which had recently become popular to ease the frequency and intensity of chronic nightmares, at a dose of between 1mg to 13mg per day. He pointed out that when taken before bedtime, this medication worked by greatly inhibiting the body's response to norepinephrine (adrenaline). This resulted in reduced frequency and intensity of chronic nightmares. He told me he'd recently learned about this medication's astounding and positive side-effect at a medical conference and asked if I'd be willing to include it into my regime.

He made it clear that because the medication is an anti-hypertensive, it would lower my blood pressure. As a result, I should be cautious of rising out of bed quickly as my blood pressure might drop causing lightheadedness. After I fully understood the risks and benefits, I agreed to start at a low dose and work my way up to the target dose in a few weeks. After all, what choice did I have? With my nights already filled with screams, blood, guns and death, anything had to be better. For me it was a choice between the lesser of two evils, and I chose the drug called Prazosin or Minipress.

I've suffered from the lasting effects of nightmares on and off for more than twenty years, and almost constantly from between 2004 to 2011. Dr. Katz suggested a conservative initial dose of 2mg before bedtime for the first two weeks. By the third week and with no noticeable side effects, he increased my dose to 4mg before bedtime. By the end of the first month the frequency and intensity of my nightmares improved somewhat. Yet, I couldn't rely on these preliminary results as I often experience a normal and systematic waxing and waning of nightmares over time. By the fifth week, Dr. Katz increased my dose to 6mg at bedtime. By the end of the eighth week, there was a consistent and marked improvement in the frequency and intensity of my nightmares. To me, these were significant results, yet I remained cautiously optimistic.

It's now been two and a half years since I started taking Prazosin to reduce my nightmares. In all, my personal results are significant. I have fewer and less intense nightmares over all. Recently though, my nightmares increased again and Dr. Katz raised my dose of Prazosin to 8mg at bedtime. He indicated that Prazosin may become less effective over time, requiring a higher dose. The adjustment did the trick and my nightmares continue to be fewer and less intense.

To put this into perspective, it feels like a victory after a twenty-year-long battle against a superior force equipped with unlimited resources. And I have Dr. Katz to thank for it. I believe my association with Dr. Katz is a part of the providence that has led me to the path of enlightenment. I encourage all of you to listen and watch for the signs that will present you with your own path in the right direction. Remember however, that your journey toward a better place requires sacrifice. The question remains, are you up for the challenge?

PERSONAL QUOTES

- *I never truly lived until I lived no more. (Cover & p. 22)*

- *I'll always remember and cherish the time I spent in Heaven, and I'll never fear death when it comes to me again, for I know that it's only the beginning. (p. 9)*

- *Enlightenment is illusive and can only be received by those who ask for it and by those who are worthy to receive it. Only then will you be shown the path. (p. 11)*

- *Faith isn't a crutch used by the frail to prevent them from falling over. Faith is our mighty staff which we wield as we walk through the valley of our personal shadow of death. (p. 53)*

- *It's true that we sometimes require our staff to lean on and provide us with strength and courage, but no more than those who lack faith and lean on the truly feeble power of money. (p. 53)*

- *Take a leap of faith, because if you're not risking something, you're not truly living. (p. 53)*

- *Having faith in God means extending yourself into uncharted waters, exposing your heart and soul so others may benefit, even when it's inconvenient. (p. 58)*

- *Faith is an unwavering trust, which gives us the power to overcome any obstacle at any time. (p. 58)*

- *Perhaps true faith can only be born from the ashes of our own personal hell. (p. 58)*

- *How arrogant are we to believe we're in control of anything, much less our own destiny. All we can do is pray for God's divine guidance and follow the path Home. (p. 69)*

- *Guilt is like a putrid sludge that courses through our flesh. (p. 80)*

- *Victims have succumbed to defeat, and their spirit has been conquered and crushed. We survivors are fearless gladiators, and our spirit can never be broken. (p. 83)*

- *We survivors face life's challenges with strength and courage, and defeat is never an option. We are insulated by the Grace of God, for we are His faithful. (p. 83)*

- *Each of our personal harbingers of doom is in reality the Ark which has brought us to this unique place and given us our unique Survivor's Perspective. (p. 86)*

- *The road to Understanding must be walked with bare feet and the path is paved with shards of glass. (p. 86)*

- *The key that will open the gateway to unburden our anger can only be forged through understanding. (p. 92)*

- *Forgiveness is truly the greatest expression of revenge. (p. 95)*

- *Remember that knowledge alone is not power. Only knowledge plus action is power. (p. 100)*

- *Our only true future is today. The past is gone forever and tomorrow may never come, so pay attention to today and enjoy it. (p. 117 & 126)*

- *Brutal experience has no room for a future in which we discount the present. (p. 118)*

- *Life isn't about us; it's about God and what He can do through us. (p. 136)*

DEDICATIONS

I dedicate this book to my wife Maria. You're the grace of my life. You're my best friend, my angel from above, and the love of my life. I know in my heart that you are without question my destiny and my life mate. With your love, existence has an angelic consequence measured by the beaming warmth you send through me every second of each day of every year. Its radiance feeds my soul with the love of a thousand loves, with the strength of a thousand men, and with the peace of a thousand angels. You're the silver lining that brought my life back from the brink. Through you, I'm blessed with a beautiful and loving woman who's stood by my side for twenty years, even when I didn't deserve it. You're the reason I wake up each morning. You make every day better. Maria, you're my salvation and I couldn't imagine a single day without you. You must know that I'm more in love with you today than ever before. Thank you for all you encouragement and support.

My love and angel, I know you feel displaced by the magnitude and significance of the events which occurred before we met. To this I can only say, you're my inspiration and my purpose for being, and life without you would surely be my death sentence. So while these events in my life hold great significance, I couldn't have written this book without the touch of your hand in mine. I'll be yours forever.

I dedicate my life to Jesus Christ and to Our Lady of Mercy, who stood before me in death and offered me a second life. I thank you both, with all that I am, for the gifts you've bestowed on me. I thank you Lord for my success and happiness, but also for my failure and sorrow. I now understand that all my experiences, both good and bad, have made me the person I am today. For how can I become more than I was before, unless my missteps teach me to. I owe my entire existence to you my God and to you Mother Mary. Thank you for teaching me how to hear your wisdom as you spoke to me through signs, thoughts, and feelings. And thank you for giving me the courage to act so I may continue to help those who need you even more than I do.

Maria and I are truly blessed with even more great riches, and their names are Adam, Jessica and Stephen. Adam, thank you for reminding me about the value that focus and determination has while perusing our dreams. Jessica, thank you for reminding me that laughter is by far the most powerful medicine. Stephen, thank you for reminding me that creativity and originality is its own reward. Thank you kids for rewarding me each day with your love, compassion and laughter. I thank you for giving me strength when I needed it most and for inspiring me to write this story. I hope it will offer faith to those who've lost theirs, strength to those who cannot bear another day of anguish, and comfort to those who feel they're all alone.

I thank my wonderful parents, Tom and Gerry, for raising me well and leading me down the righteous path. When tragedy struck me down, they never left my bedside. They expended their own spirit and tirelessly brought me hope, strength, and love. For 77 days, they prayed vigorously to keep me alive. My Mom and Dad saved my life. Thank you both for teaching me the value of a strong mind and a happy heart, even in the face of adversity.

I offer my most sincere gratitude to my brothers, Tom and Pete. Thanks for always listening with an open mind and an open heart, when I needed to vent. Thank you both for standing by my bedside and simply holding my hand, when I didn't even have the strength to speak. Please know that your strength and tenderness helped me to survive. I thank Pete for teaching me the value of perseverance even against unimaginable odds and I thank Tom, for teaching me that living life without excitement is like living a slow death.

I thank the emergency medical technicians and all the doctors and nurses who worked to keep me alive through the darkest 77 days of my life.

Next, I want to thank two friends who I call brothers, Mike Doner and Ron Duswalt. For more than thirty years, we've laughed, cried, fought, worked and sometimes bled together. We've remained the closest of friends, even over great distances. Over time, one element remains constant and keeps our friendship strong. When one of us needs help, we stop what we're doing and sometimes travel thousands of miles to come to the other's aid. This unbreakable bond is what keeps our friendship strong. Thank you both for the advice you gave in making this book a reality. Mike and Ron, thank you for offering me your blood, sweat and tears when I needed it most.

I can never fully express my sincere gratitude to the Lettiere Family for all that you've done. Jenmarie, your heroic actions will always be sweetly remembered and I'm proud to call you my friend. Uncle Joe, you're one of the greatest men I've ever had the privilege of knowing. The love and support you selflessly offered brought strength to our family in our most grievous time. I'll always love you and I'll never forget you. I'll see you on the other side; pour a glass of wine for me.

I offer my most sincere thanks to my cousins Anthony Antonucci, John Antonucci and Susan & Ernie Sangirardi for the emotional support you gave to my family in our most dire time. Sue, I want you to know that you've become the Sister I never had and that you inspire me to become a better person. You're a survivor and a hero on so many levels, and I'll always love you.

From the days of working at the Palasciano Ice Company in Brooklyn, NY, one extremely kind man stands out above the others, Mr. Bill Rice. We all called him Mr. Bill out of respect for his stature, kindness and good nature. Bill, I'm proud to call you my friend. I'll always remember your sincere and heartfelt concern. I hope you're not working too hard in that big Icehouse in the sky.

I thank all my friends from The Bank of New York®. Your heartfelt well wishes, visits, and hundreds of get-well cards gave me daily purpose and kept me focused on the positive. The impact your sentiments had was immeasurable and sustaining. Special thanks to Ed O'Donnell and Dick Crowley for your friendship and never-ending support. You've both been a beacon of guiding light and a shining example of all that is good.

This book is written in remembrance of Dick Crowley. You'll always be my friend and you'll forever be remembered in my daily thoughts and prayers.

ACKNOWLEDGEMENTS

T hank you to all my Advance Readers for being an integral part of shaping this work into a completed creation. I appreciate all the valuable time that you took out of your busy schedules. All of your incisive comments, keen editing, and creative ideas helped to make this work a reality.

Including:
Mike Doner, Chris Buckley, Paul Mila, Maria Lena Franco, Ron Duswalt, Mom & Dad, Monsignor Thomas Costa, Joy Forrler, Sue Sangirardi, Ed O'Donnell, Dr. Anthony DeRiggi, Dr. Jack Katz, Adam Palasciano, and of course, My Angel Maria.

EPILOGUE

Writing this book has certainly been a transformative experience. I see everything differently now than I did before. Before, there were hundreds of pieces of feelings and thoughts floating in my mind, like an unmade jigsaw puzzle. Over time and by putting these thoughts and feelings to paper, the puzzle has coalesced into a singular formation of truth and faith.

This process has given me clarity and has transformed a hundred separate thoughts with a hundred separate questions into a singular picture. I get it. I know why at the age of twenty seven I had to be in the best physical shape of my life. I realize why I hesitated from opening the bank on that cold November morning. I understand now that I wasn't in the wrong place at the wrong time; I was in the right place at the right time. I understand why I had to be shot and why I had to witness the shooting of my two co-workers, helpless to offer assistance. I can now appreciate why it was necessary to experience death, and why I was sent back from Heaven. I can now appreciate the significance of the wondrous gift offered to me by Our Lady of Mercy. I realize the identity of the mysterious man who entered the surgical intensive care unit, walked into my hospital room and said to me, *"You're not supposed to be here. You were chosen for a purpose, and you must find out what it is."*

I'm now aware of why it was imperative to endure nearly constant unbearable physical pain from seemingly countless surgeries as well as prolonged emotional suffering. I recognize and comprehend the words that God spoke to me when I asked him to stop my suffering. I realize why the Olive Skinned Man had so much horrific anger. Finally, I understand how and why my own anger and hatred for him has completely transformed and resolved to forgiveness, and even gratitude.

I'm compelled to pen these experiences, thoughts, and feelings, for the benefit of others who've yet to resolve their own tragedies into understanding and peace. It's my hope this work will serve as a guide to anyone who can benefit from the power of the Holy Spirit. I believe I've been shown the glory of God for a purpose, and I also believe that this work is only the beginning of my purpose.

I'll leave you with one last question. What's the most precious possession you cannot afford to lose, the foundation upon which all others are formed? Personally, my most valuable possession, that which defines me, is most certainly my faith in God.

I thank you for your consideration,
and may God be with you.

THE END?